THE FEMININE PROTOCOL

How to turn your why's? into wisdom.

ANNETTE ROSE

Spiritual Anthropologist

authorHOUSE®

AuthorHouse™ UK
1663 Liberty Drive
Bloomington, IN 47403 USA
www.authorhouse.co.uk
Phone: UK TFN: 0800 0148641 (Toll Free inside the UK)
*   UK Local: 02036 956322 (+44 20 3695 6322 from outside the UK)*

Published by AuthorHouse: 01/26/2021

ISBN: 978-1-6655-8486-9 (sc)
ISBN: 978-1-6655-8487-6 (hc)
ISBN: 978-1-6655-8485-2 (e)

CONTENTS

ABOUT THE AUTHOR

Annette wondered what her bizarre life was about. So many levels did not make sense to her. Then at the age of 40, she had a privileged experience that transformed her thinking. An alternative world that led to answers. Her own life made sense to her, she found happiness in those answers and could have used those answers in a way that would have seen her abundant in all aspects of life, but she could not accept her new found knowledge should be to keep to herself. What she had found out, she believes every woman should know. So she had to go right back to the beginning and start again, forging a path of her own so she could inspire all women, and lead them out of the misery into a new understanding and strength through re-education of the senses, as she puts it, our birthright for being born female, that has been abused since the inception of intelligent human existence.

PREFACE

Hello!

Gosh, I have waited such a long time to speak to you like this! How are you? How have you been coping?

First and foremost, I want to make it absolutely clear to you all that I am not a professional writer by any means! I have written this because it needs to be said and you need to know it.

Owing to a series of events taking place in my life, I have found a world where language is felt; no words need to be spoken. Decisions are made by what is right; money plays no part in providing happiness and contentment. There are no troubled minds, because true wisdom is always found. There is only one rule: everyone takes responsibility for his or her own actions at all times. Because of this requirement, what rules is a primary code of morals and a deep sense of honour in everything we do. Where did I find this world, this state of being?

It actually lives in our subconscious, but it rarely gets a chance to be seen. It is the world your soul believes you are living in, and it is still running with that assumption. Its rules were set out for human incarnation, before we actually arrived on earth, and no one knows any different until around three days before one passes from this earth, when one meets one's soul in readiness and feels, sees, and understands the way things *should* have been, by which time it is too late to do anything about changing things. It was finding the link to the way this world is now, to what it could and should be like, that was my unknown task at the beginning of my journey.

The direct link to the soul frequency was known primarily by the female species, as we have the ability for instinct and intuition, which links directly into the soul through the heart—in other words, the emotions. We still have that ability, but we have become shadows of our former selves. We have had the original understanding wiped from our memory because of a decision made right at the beginning of intelligent life on earth. Ever since then, our strengths, our intellects, emerge as constantly having to fight for fairness and never really achieving what our main purpose is, because no one has been able to join the dots. We get so far and then get side-tracked. In this book, I give you practically everything you need to know to make sense of that highly intelligent brain of yours that often leads to self-destruction because you know there is something missing but you can't find it.

Our nature is still there: we know compassion, we always look for a way to make things right, and we take the pain of emotion in a relationship in the hope that we will be seen for our sacrifice in holding up the mental stability of our men. What we are now is what we have become. We all feel there is something wrong but cannot do anything about it because we cannot define it. I have found the *reason* why everything is in such decline. I have found a solution because I have gone into the depths of the mind to ensure that we have a real chance of reversing an *injustice* that has been proven to be valid.

I have just given you the whole crux of this book in a few paragraphs! What you read within the pages of this book is the infinite detail, in as many variations as possible, explaining to you that there is a moral code in society that needs to be reinstated—or, as it appears, instigated, for have any of us truly understood the depth and meaning of a moral code of conduct in society? Do you believe I am right? If you are not sure at the moment, you will, ladies; rest assured of that!

For you to understand how we may return to our strength and true position within the human race, it needs to be *felt*. And for that to happen, we all need to introduce it into our lives as the reality of living—each and every one of us. Discovering where to start to engage one's mind to give it a logical path of realization has taken me twenty-five years. This new way works. There is proof. Each of us has taken a road of our own and used our gift of sight, intuition, and instinct to go down a path, as we have been taught. But this does not encourage us to look at the bigger picture for humankind, as was the expectation of the gifts that being female provides as second nature. We have had the frequency of well-being removed from our natural-born instincts and replaced with a version that suits and supports man in his desire to conquer the world.

It's time to take back our equality in the best way that can have a positive outcome for us and our children and the future generations to come. I had to find a way to include every woman in this. The link is compassion, which holds the self in a moral code of conduct if allowed to do so; but that word doesn't make sense in our understanding of it. However, it is the location of the link to your God, who lives with your soul in the soul plane. He has always been there, though in a way you cannot comprehend.

The way it has been described to us is that man has the link to God and we are supposed to follow man and obey him. We have been taught to value the true meaning of compassion as sympathy, and our empathy turns into us being controlled by the soul of man in an attempt by them to keep their souls worthy of justification. Most women are well beyond keeping themselves anywhere near the true soul message, and they turn on other women in an attempt to hold on to something so deeply sacred that they do not realize what they are doing. It should never have come to this. There is so much more to tell, and this is where I change the pace and explain it more rationally, although once you get going with this book, be prepared to look for breakthroughs in your thinking. The link is there for your self-worth and confidence, but it will take time for you to see it, and that is natural after what we have all been through.

For this massive task, I have looked into religion and how it has had an effect on our lives, as well as how it links with the higher mind in metaphysics. I have tried to cover as many angles as I could possibly come up with, as well as a few I hadn't thought about. This is why this book has been so long in the making. I have tried my best not to offend, so if offence is taken, it is not of my giving.

My only intention, and the purpose of my relaying this information to you, is to try to save our hearts from any more pain and take a look through new vision in an attempt to "clean up" our spiritual path so the future of our children, and all yet to be born, have some proper guidelines in life, knowing that they are safe in society rather than fearful of what lies outside of their front door.

Even worse for some is that things happening within the home have been terrifying for their innocent souls to have to comprehend. For all of those that would harm our purity, beware. For the rest of us, we now have the backing of universal law on our side, which sees all. There are no loopholes, no rocks under which to crawl and hide. How we, meaning you, can achieve this and integrate this new alignment with the world of soul law is what this book is all about. I hope I do justice to your soul, which is my primary concern.

It is your soul that has helped me produce this publication for you to learn a better way to acknowledge your worth. Most of it is biased towards women, but the reading of it, and indeed the initiation process further into the book, can include your husband or partner in his own right if you want him to understand the messages within and help change the future for your children. It will also enhance his own well-being and your confidence to get to know him for his true masculine qualities, which are present to protect the female species, before you lose the will to fight for his worth.

Everyone I have spoken to agrees to this, because there is no better way to be able to trust without hesitation that no one would cause you harm in anyway, because no one would choose that for themselves in return. Harmony rules the senses, so peaceful solutions are always found for any conflict of interest that may look harmful. When something has caused doubt, it is nearly always misunderstanding that has got in the way somewhere.

Things can be resolved quickly without fuss, and the experience is used to make the pot of wisdom accessible for anyone looking for a better solution at a time when wisdom is needed. Sounds like an amazing place, doesn't it? Do you know where I found it? It lives in your soul, for you to find. It lives in every soul, in fact. How and why I unearthed this is what my book is about. There is no language to convey such things, as I said, so I have had to find a language—a conformity that I hope you will understand.

Your soul is crying out for you to hear this, so I made it my purpose to find you so you could hear what your soul needs you to hear. My explanations are true. I run with the primary code of the soul plane; I wouldn't have it or want it any other way. My purpose is solely to let the injustices in all of come to light, proving that we have never consciously known this level of communication and well-being.

I have worked with your soul and the souls that have wanted me to reach you for twenty-five years to ensure I could bring this to you in a language that you could understand, with the proof that you might need to hear of my words of truth and clarity. I have considered for many years how I could achieve this without being branded as deranged or deluded, of which I am neither. I am a woman, like you, that found something so disturbing about the way it has always been for women that I needed to know the truth.

Now that I know, you will know. I then had to think about how I was going to get this information to you. I came up with the simple logic of using honesty and truthfulness, laying my soul in front of you with the wisdom I have found on so many subjects. This is the only way this would work without me coming across as the newest guru in town to tell you how to reach a peaceful existence by denial, on all accounts, of your true worth.

So read on. This is what I have come up with in an effort to reach you. You need to be ready to be disturbed, shocked, and prepared to step up to becoming the true warrior that has lived inside of you since the day you were born, waiting to be heard. With my wisdom now being sufficient to bring to you, I needed to find words to write regarding how to reach those deepest parts within you that aren't used to being challenged.

Each time I sat down at the computer, I was guided to say something else that would benefit someone, even if I had already spoken of a particular angle of it previously. And that is the point. There are so many angles, points of view, but they all lead to one thing—and this is what I am trying to convey to you in my deciphering of an unspoken language that is crying out to be heard by all that will listen.

ACKNOWLEDGEMENTS

I would like to thank Nisi Grint for her help in showing me how to observe the rules of the written word and for going through the first draft of my book to give advice on the presentation of facts and to make sure that I saved my work on the computer with backups, alternative files, and things that the passion for writing sometimes overlooks. Her help was at the very inception of my writing this book, and her advice was invaluable. Thanks again, Nisi!

I would also like to mention Debbie Manning, who has been my contact at my publisher. Before I even started to write, Debbie was encouraging me to just get on with it! She was a great inspiration to me personally. She believed in me before I put pen to paper, just by hearing my words and my passion to help women everywhere. Thank you, Debbie. My success is also yours.

Also deserving of a mention is my friend Karen, who has always been there as a refreshing change to keep me grounded. She has always inspired me with her strength of character, and she found ways that I hadn't thought of to help me pursue my goal of writing this book. She is a true friend in many ways.

INTRODUCTION

I am sharing with you my life, my experiences, and what I have found out about within our role as women from outside of the normal "frequencies" that we use to think and feel. This is sometimes hard-hitting. It might be disturbing for some readers, and it will change your life forever if you choose to believe all that I have written. Sometimes (actually most of the time) my words might come across as forceful; that's my passion being delivered to you in the way that I have been given this to write. This has been brought to you now as a missing element that needs to be re-established in our minds. I call it "the feminine protocol", which you will become firm friends with by the end of this book—or, as I like to refer to it, your teaching manual.

There is no time to be pussyfooting around the knowledge that is within these pages. I feel a bit like the woman Sarah Connor from the Terminator films who had to protect her son at all costs. She would go to any lengths to get the message across that something was going to happen unless she was believed and action was taken to prevent the total collapse of the free will we were given as human beings. Likewise, I am here to re-educate you and introduce to you an alternative version of what *your* free will actually means to you.

I kid you not. The understanding I stumbled across is something I could not leave for fate to bring to your attention. I must explain what is in store for us unless we do something about it to reverse the wheels of destiny on the course we are currently set on. I could not just let it sit there in my mind without doing my best to engage with *all women* to let them know that the future of the human race is indeed in our hands and that you have the individual power to enhance your own life. More importantly, you have the power to protect the lives of your children and future generations.

This book is giving you a choice to take the information in it seriously or risk not having a choice, as your own free will be used for someone else's bidding and that of humankind within a few years—and this will occur within the universal laws set for us as being totally legal, because we will have allowed it to happen. If you choose not to take it seriously, you won't realize what could have been until a few days before it is time for you to leave this earth, by which time it will be too late for you to turn back the clock.

I apologize unreservedly for when I repeat things, or if you feel that I am talking to you in a tone that assumes command over your ultimate well-being. It all depends on how much you trust what I have to say. I hope you are at least able to allow me the benefit of the doubt. I have written this keeping in mind the most spiritually downtrodden amongst us, who live across society, mostly unseen. The intention is to make you realize that it is indeed your emotional traumas in particular that will be taken into account when universal law has its say on how you have been treated by those that dared to do so.

We collectively have the power, and I will teach you all into knowing what true freedom is. I will lead you all with inspirational talks and will speak to you—personally, if need be—if you are struggling. I will be there, walking beside you, *with* you, at every difficult step with my words. I have gone on ahead to make sure you never have to face adversity alone. You will now have the feminine protocol as a guide and protector through the teaching of how to achieve wisdom. This will allow you to be introduced to an enhanced level of awareness, and your intuition and instinct will grow as you progress on your new understanding of life.

It is time for us to take responsibility for our conduct and to own our truth. The beauty of this is that when we do this from the level I speak of in this book, the responsibility goes back down the line until it reaches the point of inception, and this is what *needs* to happen for us to regain our *lawful right* in the eyes of universal law—a largely unknown entity to most of us.

Until now, no one has been able to instigate this change of command and cover the jurisdiction that is needed to complete such a task as this. I have spent the last twenty-five years ensuring a frequency that was opened to me to access the realms that deal with justice was sound and worked—and it does. What I found there was so disturbing that I had to research my findings on many levels to confirm that the truth behind it was real, and it all pointed to one thing.

In a short, short version of events, it appears that we have been duped into underestimating our worth on such a vast scale, starting at the inception of life itself, right at the beginning of the advent of intelligent life here on earth. I have been given this opportunity to put things right, to reset the boundaries, because of my insistence and stubbornness not to let this go unnoticed and without retribution. But how does one define truth and then find a way to pass the knowledge on so it won't be abused in the future and the whole cycle of events will not start all over again? I have literally gone to the ends of the spiritual realms to follow the emotional entanglements, the "lesser than" truths, that everyone accepts without question.

I have tried my absolute hardest, from the bottom of my heart, to include everyone, and I have traversed the most diverse of experiences to help me unravel this massive set of lies that we call truth. It is with the advocacy of the fifth dimension, where the gatekeepers of the sanctity of our innermost vulnerabilities are known, that I have been guided in my quest to find the ultimate truth of the demise of our well-being and everything that we hold sacred.

The gatekeepers have backed me and supported me, and even now they continue to ensure that I reach the parts of the soul plane that I need to reach for the task I am here to do. They know change is needed, and my persistence and other understandings, which I don't need to display here, made me the perfect adversary for their input to help us understand wisdom and where to find it. Could I stay the course? Had I the patience and tolerance to succeed?

My job was to find a language that could be heard by all. I have had to learn how to decipher this wisdom, how to comprehend the right understandings that would settle a troubled mind and encourage the search in every one of us to uncover a hidden truth.

I have been taught the language of instinct and intuition, as well as the "in-between" language of graphs, shadows, percentages, and so much more. I have been allowed to do this in a way that only those who truly desire to help with the growth of humankind's abilities towards a universal moral code are allowed to see. I have learnt what it means to be a true detective and communicator of worlds. I have much to be grateful for, especially at times when my frustration means I need more patience and tolerance regarding my inability to see the link to wisdom.

In truth, the deciphering of new languages never stops. Neither does the wisdom that accompanies that learning. Tolerance and patience have to be the first commodities one learns about—and I have so much gratitude for all the masters that have lived a life on earth, and some that haven't, who ensure my safekeeping in the face of all adversity that comes my way. This allows me to bring this to you now, out in the open, for all those that are looking for peace of mind and clarity of vision to learn with the aid and rules of the fifth dimension relating to leniency and inspiration.

I have written this to inspire you, to allow you to see, and to show you how to understand the difference between pure truth, which allows true freedom, and the truth of who you are, which society *and* you accept as truth. I have done all I can possibly do to get to this point of awareness. I know the world cannot wait any longer to hear the biggest lie that sits amongst us in plain sight.

What you decide to do once you have read this book is up to you. I asked the powers that be for an opportunity to give women a chance to hear an alternative truth about their unhappiness which will make sense to their troubled minds and inspire a change of destiny. This is particularly written for those that are lacking in self-worth, have low self-esteem, are depressed, have habits they can't kick, or are even struggling just to stay alive under the pressures that appear to be imposed on their shattered souls. Once realigned with the proper sensory instruction, all diseases and all I have mentioned above will gradually disappear.

The soul will no longer need to send messages that are misinterpreted by your body and lead to disharmony and possibly serious disease. But you have had no way until now to know how to decipher these messages. Now you have an opportunity to sharpen your toolbox of intelligence and find that intellect that can communicate with your spiritual thread that is your link to well-being. Your soul can breathe fresh air again instead of recycling old, spent air that just keeps you incarnate as your soul cries out in despair to be heard by you.

Then there are those that are strong, but in a way that has had to allow their masculine intelligence to rule, not allowing their feminine skills to surface for fear of them appearing vulnerable. But how would you know the difference? How can you tell? How can you change the story of you? This book is science meeting intuition, meeting clairvoyance, meeting instinct, meeting everyday life. It is a new emotional integrity that will increase your awareness of who and what you are, and your perceptions of what life could be for you.

The reason why this book was twenty-five years in the making is mainly because there are so many levels of awareness that are possible. I had to decipher the ones that would inspire. There are so many levels of subconscious weighing up on every decision we make, every action we take, and every word we speak. It might seem a bit higgledy-piggledy in its presentation—apologies for that again in advance. Speaking about a subject face to face with interaction is so much easier to relay than one level of the written word at a time. But all levels reach the same conclusion.

In hindsight, I suppose that I have written about things as they became important to write about—perhaps when I had the sudden thought, *I must mention that; it might mean something to someone and help him or her in some way.* It was a complex task to determine how to inspire you and how to let you know a truth so far reaching you would have to open your mind up to levels possibly unknown to you before. And I had to do this for a multi-layered population—that of the entire world. For those that like a study of something that is certified, I can provide that too! Under the reiki tradition, I have combined reiki into this, as I understood I could reach levels I had already visited five years previously, with the right determination and intention.

This covered the aspects of universal law that I had already reached and that could not be refuted, to ensure a particular kind of energy flow was "legally" able to be used by me, according to universal law. It also has the ability to override the masculine "taught" energy so we can be at one with its proper time of use. This, in its own way of natural law through the feminine protocol, ensures it allows your feminine energy to be taken back to a state of purity so it can receive new tuition that will enhance a new oneness through natural wisdom.

While my initial reiki initiation was being done, I was taken to a frequency that I understood was mine alone to find, because of the work I was destined to do. I then used this level of integrity to access the parts of the soul plane that I needed to access. I had thrown down the spiritual gauntlet to bring our worth as women into recovery.

I needed the ammunition of wisdom, which was required to bring true peace and harmony into a world that thrives on the fear of ill-equipped, vulnerable minds that have been letting strong minds rule our senses without being interviewed for their intention and purpose for our well-being. I was given the green light regarding my purpose, and the way was cleared for me to achieve all that I needed to.

In this regard, Dr Usui, the founder of reiki in our recent historical time frame, has been ensuring that I pushed my own research as much as he pushed his own, but in a different way, so as to ensure the success of my study and knowledge. He provided me personally with a unique vehicle to access all levels and the fifth dimension so I could have clarity in my mind on exactly what it was I had in my possession—something I couldn't understand because there was no one like me with the knowledge I had at that point.

I have had to be ready to face all challenges thrown my way and to see how I would react to adversity in many situations of life. I have had harsh training on all aspects of emotional response levels, knowing I had to seek the advice of the highest wisdom, from the knowledge of what was happening. In so doing, I have been given as my reward the code of life itself, as well as a way of passing it on for all those willing to take on the challenge of changing, or upgrading, the thought patterns of women so a new destiny can be found for us, for our children, and for the future of humankind.

Finally, what kept me going (and still keeps me going) was thinking about every person going through the same distress I had gone through. At that point of exasperation in my life, that lowest point, I had no one to turn to or to talk to who would see the real me inside, racked with torment. I didn't want to put myself out there as needing help, because nobody could help me.

You see, because I was considered to be an intelligent woman, no one would have believed me if I had told them of my torments. I have written this for you, as I believe we all feel like this at some point in our lives, to various extremes. I would like to think that you see me as an unseen, unknown friend that only you know about. I am your secret in a world that likes to gossip about the demise of a soul and finds pleasure in doing that.

I hope I stack up to your expectations of a friend in deeds—one who is there for you when you can't be.

This is an opportunity to make sense of those thoughts that *don't* make sense, deep down. This will allow you to sleep at night, because you will actually feel at one with yourself and the world. A peaceful mind is one that knows and lives in harmony because it has learnt how to find emotional control on a level that overrides the world of fear and torment. I teach you how to reach that state of bliss whilst keeping your feet on the ground.

You will never feel alone again either, should you decide to take my words seriously. You will also have eternal gratitude from all women that have passed from this life without being heard. They will know that their passing will not have been in vain.

To reason with and validate our emotions that assist us in

our decision-making is so important. There has never been an understanding like this one. Once you have understood the concept of what I say, it is the implementation of its meaning to *you* that will change your world. The original misconception of who women are as dictated by religious understandings having been dealt with in this book. We can now go forward with our lives with a whole new strength of attitude towards our feminine selves and the confidence that brings when used in its fullness of wisdom.

In the bigger picture, my extended aim is for a version of this to be taught in schools so children have a better understanding that life is built on the basic rules of good manners, good morals, respect, and honour through a moral code of conduct. If these elements were taught across the world in the same way as the first port of call in education, there would be little disharmony in the world. Today's children are tomorrow's adults, tomorrow's politicians, and tomorrow's leaders.

For the academics amongst us, there has been a global spiritual sensory displacement that affects every decision that we make, due to an error of judgement made at the very beginning of intelligent life, when the rules on conduct were set in stone. Emotional entanglement of the senses is rife, and this is the cause of relationship problems, depression, suicidal tendencies, addictions, unwanted weight gain, illness, and disease. In short, we have been lacking spiritual well-being from a soul perspective, which has in turn affected our physical well-being.

There is nothing difficult about this; it just needs the determination of those in power now to be determined and positive in their desire for true human worth to be a global entity. I am always here to discuss the way this could be applied in schools for children of all denominations and ages. There is no excuse for why the children of today and tomorrow should have to live in a world without true guidelines that respect and honour all life forms in a new way of understanding.

Time is one thing children have in their favour. It is up to us to ensure that wisdom, not knowledge, is the ultimate purpose of any teaching. This in itself will alter the benchmark of the society they will grow up in, as they will eventually be in control of it. You see, we have all been suffering from spiritual sensory displacement, meaning we have lost the ability to see what is really important in life. This has been brought on by emotional entanglement due to an unforeseen flaw in the original rules of conduct and behaviour.

For instance, what we have been led to believe is important in life is usually not realized until it is far too late to change things. I will explain this very complex subject to the best of my ability, but trying to cover as many angles as possible to show you why and how this has happened has by no means been an easy task. The important thing to know is that it *has* happened and will *continue* to happen unless we do something positive to put right the incorrect teachings of our ancestors, which goes back to the very beginning of the Bible and most religious teachings.

I have aimed this new way of being for women, because we are the ones that gave our innocence in trust away. Another word for innocence is "purity", and this very element is the crux of the problem. So we need to collectively take back our birthright as it should always have been. I will explained this further throughout this book. This is the first step to a new way of thinking. It is time for this depravation of soul worth to be given a full belly of true nourishment of well-being that will last a lifetime.

Once you have understood this new concept, the children need to be taught this new way so they will not have to suffer as we have. For the first time, a refreshing change of ideas with a moral code could be taught easily. But to start with, we have to acknowledge how vastly and widely this unknown secret has affected our lives so we can insist on changing the first element of teaching personal life skills, which must occur before any other education can take place. It is the foundation of every subject taught and will enhance learning skills throughout every life on the planet. We are supposed to be intelligent beings. It is time to show the world what we are really prepared to do to when it comes to pulling together and ensuring a better future for ourselves and the futures of our children. It is time for women to truly regain our worth from every aspect, with total respect for our femininity—the most powerful force on earth—and then assume the responsibility of using this power. Read this once, and then read it again. Be sure you understand the potential of this information and how it will change your life forever. It did mine.

1

THE BEGINNING OF A NEW LIFE

It all started on 19 December 1994.

Consciously, that is. That night, I had a real-time vision that I was being blessed by someone.

Upon awakening, I had my hand across my forehead, whereas in my vision, the hand had been that of an elderly man from the Orient. From that moment on, I have felt I am a part of something much bigger than just me—a single mother of three daughters struggling in a world that still sees single mothers as some sort of failure which does not fit in with the two-parent family ideal. But no one knows what goes on behind closed doors, do they? No one sees the control, the abuse, and the unhappiness of trying to live a life of "fitting in" when it is a total lie to the truth of one's soul.

I have slightly digressed. However, occasionally the truth sends me on a tangent of gritty emotion that takes me away from what I have to tell you. This is my story of how I got to this place of knowing that I wasn't just here for me.

I think it is wise to tell you about my journey to this portal of understanding knowledge and wisdom, and of learning how to tell the difference between the two. I would probably want to hear my story if I were in your shoes so I could know you had been through what I either am going through or have been going through in my life up till now.

The one thing I do know is that you would not be reading this if you were not meant to. It might be that you have reached that point of total, utter despair that leaves you not knowing who you are any more, and you cannot find a reason for continuing this desperately unhappy life the way it is going for you right now. Perhaps you have heard all the answers that others have given you, and nothing has quite fit your mindset to help you see any different. Maybe you don't know what it is that's wrong, but nothing is pulling you out of the intense misery and self-sabotage that surrounds you as the only sensible option.

Or it could be that it's not you that is going through it. It might be someone you know that you so want to help.

One thing I do want to make abundantly clear is that I have brought this to you now because it is time.

I understood that there was a world out there that I hadn't explored yet because no one teaches us how to understand the language of the soul. The *interpretation* is missing in our mind's vocabulary process to explain that we should not have to feel alone, powerless, or frustrated at not being heard for the intelligence (yes, intelligence, but we do not see it as that) that we know no one else gets, which makes it look as though we are going mad and beyond help.

I wondered at my deepest and most desperate moments what other women did at this lowest point of emotional turmoil?

Alone, I cried out for help, shouting out that something had to be wrong. Why was I having to endure such pain? In that moment, everything went still. I felt a calmness and an overwhelming sense that I had to do something about changing the way things looked to be destined for me and for women going through such turmoil.

Suddenly my mind was opened to the fact that I was going to start something so huge that the world would have to listen. I was able to understand that it wasn't me that had got it wrong on what life is all about.

I did not know (nor would I have understood) of the levels, depths, and time this would take. I have been on a journey to ensure I understood all the laws that guide us. (I didn't even know that there were laws.) I went further because I had to. What I did not know at the inception was what I would uncover on my journey to find the ultimate truth of unhappiness. It wasn't at all what I believed it would be. No one could be ready for this truth. I know I certainly wasn't.

If you treat this book as though you have been given an enormous task to find answers that go deep into your subconscious, transcending emotion, thought, and logic, to find a deeper understanding of yourself and who you are, this will be the most beneficial approach. You will be taught a new and evolving language whilst en-route. This book will be your companion and guide on your journey, there to let you know that it isn't you that's got it wrong. It will be like, "Yes! I knew it! It *isn't* me," as the answers you come up with for your own life suddenly *do* make perfect sense to you.

You see, although this is my journey, the actual process and its findings relate to every one of us. It's just different drama in each of our lives. The system, it appears, has been produced to ensure we remain individuals, without realizing who we actually are, and this raw sense of understanding relates to every female born.

It all started because my life just didn't make sense to me.

Things started to happen to me which were so bizarre that I found myself going deeper and deeper within my consciousness, continuing to ask "Why?" and challenging the answers that were imprinted in my "normal" response and attitude as a woman. Make no mistake; this was not an easy task, as my mind was trying to convince me that my thoughts about who I was as a person so far were the right ones, and it was I that was trying too hard to think outside the box, which was futile.

But there was a sensibility in a new thought pattern that had surfaced in my mind. What if I had got it wrong all these years? What if my new-found thoughts were right and there was a level of consciousness that went beyond what I had been given to believe was the story of me?

In the reality of the world that everyone saw, I was a single woman with three children. I was shunned by society and open to offers from every man who realized I was no longer attached. I was living off benefits, as my ex had made sure that my business was shut down by spreading rumours that I was not a reputable person to do business with.

The next two years found me fighting my conscience about my own behaviour, which was not that of a mother, so much, but that of a woman, alone. My husband had been everything that a woman craving demonstrative love (as I was so desperate for) could ever want. But I had made the fatal mistake of giving him my trust. He used and abused that trust, and I now had to recover from that. I had to decipher which actions and decisions were mine and which were the ones I had been taught and coerced into believing were mine.

These two years of wandering in the wilderness of trying to find the right direction were hard. I am not proud of who I was before my mind was opened to who I had become. I knew I didn't like myself, but I had no guidance on how to get out of the thought pattern that I had to prove I was still desirable to men and was not a failure. I believed I was in control, but that was far from the truth.

I became a pawn in the game of life, being taken at any moment that a man showed me attention. The commodity was my body, and I had been taught how to use it. As I said, as a woman, these were hard times.

As a mother, my life and the lives of my children blossomed. They were far happier, and gradually my worth as a mother outweighed that of my personal pride of being a woman.

So, swiftly moving on, between 1994 and 1996, my whole concept changed. These, too, were very hard times of personal growth. At least this time I was self-cleansing (as best I can put it) of the person I had become. I had self-loathing, and I threw all my clothes away that reminded me of the person I had been in those wilderness years of soul destruction. I began to be able to separate my emotional field of the person that I had become from that of the person I once was. My self-respect grew, and my entanglements were easier to spot.

I found a new level of consciousness that found me wanting to write down my struggles, and I started to ask for help from within in overcoming the trauma of familiar haunts that troubled me. I continued to write until an answer presented itself that solved that dilemma. What was happening to me as a person without realizing it was that I was becoming stronger spiritually. I did not know that term then; I was just me, but I was feeling more alive each time before I again took a dive into bad thoughts.

Gradually, the new good thought processes outweighed the bad as I learned new techniques to block my old habit of thinking I was a bad person, which then spiralled into "dark" thinking (e.g., that I couldn't do this and was not going to be able to maintain this new me that was emerging). It was always my choice to rise above old habits.

My determination and stubbornness in refusing to go back to that dark place of feeling unworthy of anything good started to gain ground over the sad, pathetic woman under society's version of me that I had become.

I began to see the trigger points and the mistrust that I had for people in my life at that time who didn't really know me. It was then that I started to challenge my own understanding of what I was finding when I entered this new level of consciousness, which was becoming more the norm for me than the everyday version of what life was for me.

I was even challenging the help I was being offered spiritually at one point. Confidence can overtake it if you push hard enough, for the right reason. There are many women that live in piety—society's version of being a "good" woman—and it stays at that. This is not where it is meant to be left at—unless you choose that way once you have all the facts in your possession.

Don't worry; I have experienced all you need to understand on the deepest levels for you. Obviously you will want to check things out for yourself, but if you can justify my story to your mind, believe in it, and run with its findings for and in your own journey, you won't have to visit Mrs Piety for long (if at all) before you step forward into true worthiness of designing your own version of perfection.

To briefly recap, I was challenging a world that, in my new understanding, made more sense of whom I was evolving into. It had pulled me out of the pathetic person I had become. But I still had the deep-rooted feeling that there was something being kept from me.

A greater level was there that I wanted—or should I say *needed*—to explore for my own curiosity because some things about myself were being uncovered that didn't make sense to me.

As I said, I found myself continually persecuting who I was—but I was not being allowed to go further into who I was *before* I was with my second husband, which was where all of the self-respect issues surfaced. When I was with my first husband, I was pure. I was the perfect wife. I was living my life in a closed world of being pure of thought and deed.

I understood the price of being with someone that I felt respected by as a person—probably too much so—but I was not seen as someone to have sex with (details on that in a bit). I was still a virgin throughout the eighteen years I spent with my first husband. I resisted the many attentions of other men I naturally crossed paths with. I remained faithful and loyal throughout those eighteen years.

Why was *that* never being allowed to come into my thoughts as a balance? Why was it only this side of me that was constantly under scrutiny, being judged for who I was then? Why was the *reason* my patterns of behaviour had changed not being taken into account? This happened due to the perverted teachings of my second husband. Was it due to my being a naive, vulnerable soul then? It was only thoughts of persecution for being a 'harlot' and a bad person that continued to plague me, although I had long since (two years past) given up that way of life.

I felt something was wrong. I was being taken on a continual loop of self-persecution. But this level of spiritual acceptance was still better than the lonely person I had become to ensure I could not be physically drawn back into the world of debauchery that had become the story of me. What happened next as I challenged my thoughts further changed my life forever.

I cannot tell you why this happened or how all this started in this depth, but I am going to explain what happened, and you can make of it what you will.

By August 1996, I had got used to tuning in to a frequency outside of normal logical deep thinking. (That's the best I can do to describe it; it is like tuning into a radio station with the mind.) Suddenly I was taken to a place similar to a circus ring in structure. I was outside the ring, watching people walking around in circles, seemingly aimlessly. Then I recognized someone right in the middle, and I caught his eye simultaneously.

I felt that I knew this man. I recognized him as being Jesus personified. (He looked just like the paintings that depict him for all to see). He beckoned me to come to him. I looked behind me, thinking it must be someone else he was trying to get the attention of, but it was me. He beckoned a second time. I stepped over the border of the circus ring and walked towards him.

As I got closer, he ushered me to pass in front of him and to go to the other side of the ring. As I physically passed him, I could feel an amazing force, which I can only describe as magnetic, between us. It was similar to the magnetic force you can feel when two magnets come into contact with each other.

I can still feel that feeling today, as I write this. Anyway, as soon as I had passed him, I found myself inside a large ancient building that I found reminiscent of a palace, with black-and-white marble flooring. There were big, ornate, round white pillars from floor to ceiling at various points. As I carried on walking, I saw that I was approaching a layout that one might see in a courtroom, with a jury present. What I did not know then was that this was the Universal Court of Law.

There were nine persons (I felt only male beings present) in two rows: four on the bottom row, and five on the row above. For some reason, I felt mistrust in one of them; it seemed that they were looking at me too closely. Whatever the meaning of that thought was, I have no idea, but it made me feel as though I didn't, and couldn't, trust him. Then I looked to the left and saw what I believed (most unexpectedly) to be God sitting on a throne, just as a judge would be, as far as positioning went. I fell to the floor, feeling unworthy of being there. He told me to stand up and speak. I said, "I do want to speak to you, but in private, not in front of them."

He smiled, came down from his throne, and beckoned for me to follow him into a room which had a big oak door. When we entered, I looked around this magnificent room, with its tall ceilings and high windows. As I looked round the room, walking further into it, I was in awe of the magnificent high ceilings and the lovely green brocade curtain.

He then spoke to me, saying, "My daughter, you have found me."

I turned to face him, confused at this statement, and saw that he had his arms outstretched, ready for me to go to him for a hug. At this point I physically pulled out of my "frequency state," stood up, and rushed to my bedroom door to get out of there, though I had no idea where I was going to go!. As I got to the door, I felt a presence of many angels—or cherubs, call them what you will—holding the door closed. They said to me, "Where are you going?"

I said, "Did you just hear what he said? He thinks I am his daughter!"

They replied, "And what if you are? What have you got to lose by listening to him and what he has to say?" I thought this was a logical statement, so I went back to where I was, again tuning in to that frequency.

For the next six weeks, after the children had gone to bed, I would sit in my special place and tune in to the frequency that took me straight into that room. He would be sitting in a green velvet comfy fireside chair, and I would sit on the floor to the right of him, with my head resting on his lap, and he would stroke my head.

We chatted all night, and quite often it would be 5:00 a.m. before I came out of that frequency. Over this time I had many wisdoms imprinted into my mind; I understood everything. At one point in time, during the day, my mind was running in six dimensions all at the same time, simultaneously. I couldn't take it for long. After about three weeks, I shouted "*Stop!* I can't do this any longer; it's too much to cope with."

Something else happened too, whilst I sat each day, reflecting on the vast amount of information that had been given to me. I had this niggling thought that "God", as we know him, had been, for want of a better term, captured and was being held prisoner in another level of communication. This might seem the most out-there statement of this entire book, and I hesitated before writing this part.

But what if this thought was true? Why was I thinking this? More to the point, *who* was keeping God a prisoner? And *why?* Let alone the most troubling thought of all—*How?* It didn't matter how much I tried to counteract this thought with an another easier-to-live-with lie. Everything pointed to this most bizarre, out-there conclusion that I wasn't wrong.

So I vowed then that I would find the answer to this ridiculous but true deep instinct of mine that something was badly wrong. I committed myself through choice and had the mammoth task of finding answers to questions I didn't even know were there to be asked. How does one enter that mindset of effectively taking on the world alone, because I knew in my heart of hearts that what I had stumbled across was a truth so vast in its outcome that I had to be very sure what I was finding out about was true to the very essence of human consciousness. I had to be willing to uncover clues that I could bring to the world with confidence and strength in knowing I was right, no matter how long it took.

But before I could even do this, I had to go through a certain protocol that exists for every human being that has sought and been granted access to the highest realms of consciousness through his or her own endeavours to gain insight into truths that are not available for those that choose to follow through trust of the religions of others who dictate the way it is to be for people.

I had to go right back to the beginning, looking through fresh eyes at information as it has been written for us on how we are to conduct ourselves. I had to use what was available in the way of history books, religious books, and philosophical writings, and read between the lines of what man has written for us to be guided by. I even progressed to scientific matter regarding dimensions, DNA structures, and other information. My understanding grew, and I was able to read between the lines on just about every bit of information I was laying my hands on.

Gradually, a whole new concept was forming—one that not only proved my theory but went even further than what I had anticipated would be the outcome. It was a matter of cause and effect on the subtlest of details. It is all there to be seen in plain sight by the eye of the true spiritual detective. There was also a far bigger picture that was continuing to emerge that I just couldn't ignore, as it kept surfacing in relation to the cause of humankind's problems.

My instinctual understanding that God had been captured was right. How many times do you hear people saying, "If there is a God, why does he let bad things happen in the world?"

Could it be that God has not had free rein on our behaviour and our conduct towards each other, as he would like, because man's version of God through religion has circumvented *his* choice to intervene?

Might it be that we, as a species, have given our trust to human deliverance through religion rather than keeping our trust in God as a separate being in his own right? Have we downgraded God to a being whom man has created, through religion, in a bid to "own" God and what he is capable of? If this is the case, is this some big plan, or is it a misconception? In other words, was the act premeditated, or was it an act of misconception or naivety?

Looking at my version of this, just for a moment, could it be that God himself is being stopped from reaching you directly because we have been indoctrinated into thinking that religion, per se, has the connection and that we have to go through the religious teachings of man to reach any sort of peace of mind?

This is complexity itself. It needed total and thorough investigation. It needed compassion. It needed insight but had to be delivered through foresight. I needed to research, to go into the history of man right from the beginning, looking for the clues from a *specific* viewpoint—one that is hidden but is in plain sight if you care to dig deep enough into the unspoken history of the human race.

I have given you insight into a point in our history where decisions had to be made, and unfortunately the wrong level of approach was applied. I cannot possibly give you all of the details of my research on every point in our known history. But the evidence that supports my view to follow is part of religious record. I have looked at what is written so as to be able to decipher what is *not* written.

Out of interest, I have applied the same logic to this as I have to my clients, but posthumously. I have never had to go back so far in history, though, to find answers! But it all makes simple, logical sense. The time is now for us all to know this information. What you do with it, as always, is up to you. I have researched this to inspire you to search for your own answers and see whether this makes sense to you. It certainly fits in with a soul logic that has been waiting to be uncovered.

I was given pointers on where to look, providing I kept my intuition clear and focused. I did it all from a viewpoint of cause and effect on the lives that have changed our world in history. I was also prompted in subtle ways to look at people that have changed history without being acknowledged for it, because no one would otherwise give a thought to looking at them; nor would someone know what to look *for*.

The clues are always there if you know which method to apply and how to apply it. The depth of my answer was so simple, but it needed a concentration of *everything* I had learned on my journey to be looked at simultaneously whilst slowing down time in its own right, because I continued to miss something *so important,* but I didn't know what I was looking for as to the original cause.

It was important for me to keep God in my mind the way I had got to know him. I knew there was something wrong. There was a piece of the jigsaw puzzle that I hadn't got. The way he and universal law had personally treated me was so vastly different from the world I physically live in. And what was the point in that? There was such a divide between what was expected of me as a woman and what was expected of me as a mother in this physical world, which was nearly impossible for me to uphold in the metaphysical world, where I had learnt that everything is harmonious and the only desire is that of well-being and harmony.

I found ways to attain what I needed to. I also found balance in time so I could live in two worlds simultaneously; thus I could continue with my mission. There have been difficult times when I have had to take the lead on sacrifice, but I have always been given wisdom to see me through the darkest moments. You see, something was imprinted in my mind as to the answer, but this would be revealed to me only when I had enough knowledge, wisdom, and persistence to find the truth.

The truth is that God was his *own* prisoner, out of choice, to protect man from himself. But God was imprisoning himself on a level to see whether humankind could search for a wisdom that was hidden, and if one really believed, one would find it. The reality of this is that *man* would never find it; it had to be a woman. Men would not need to find it, as ego to them would mean they had got it wrong, and that would mean going against long-held beliefs that they do not need to challenge.

They also, in truth, would not know where to start looking, even if they wanted to try to put things on an equal footing. Many men are gurus and have the following of many women, but they still hold the power of superiority over their followers by not allowing a truth that should be known to them if they truly wanted to give back the soul worth to their female clients. Why doesn't this happen? Because they are dealing only with the *effect* of emotional trauma, not the real *cause* of it. And this is the case for most healers, life-coaches, counsellors, and therapists. I must stress that it is not their fault that they don't know the answers. Education, and the qualifications they need to carry out their desired vocation, does not require the depth of this research and would not have been taught to them.

No one wants to do the journey, because it means going deep into one's own life for the ultimate answers and then being prepared to go to great lengths for one's clients to be able to find answers for themselves too. This I bring to you now on the level at which I have understood it, and I will endeavour, as always, to bring it to you in simple language in the hope you will interpret it within your own reasoning and agree with the conclusion I have arrived at. I do hope so, as then we can work together in greater numbers. So here it is—the ultimate answer that will solve most of our problems. How much of this understanding makes sense to you only you can decide.

We now turn our attention to Moses (from the bible) as a person. When he was on the mountain having the rules dictated by God, Moses was on a spiritual level, totally at one with what needed to be conveyed. God dictated the common rules of living in unity, harmoniously. It is written that when he returned from the mountain, the people were "worshipping idols", and a golden calf was one of them.

Now, this exact point is where it happened, this misconception of truth, if you slow down time the way I have. Moses was furious, upset, and distraught. He felt betrayed by the people for everything he had gone through, and he felt that God had been belittled, defiled, and dishonoured, and he felt all of these emotions as though they were his. He was using his *free will*, albeit unwittingly, in that moment. He felt betrayed by the people, for the journey he had undertaken for his people deserved far more respect than this. It is written, that in this moment, he smashed the stones. He then had to ask God to help him rewrite them. God said, "No, you write them; you know what you were told to write."

Two things happened here. First, a man was being told to take responsibility for writing the rules as he remembered them. We must take into account that Moses had just experienced emotional turmoil, disgust, betrayal, and probably anger. The people that he thought he knew before he went up the mountain, whom he was doing this for, had changed when left to their own devices, unchecked. So Moses would have written the rules as a changed person himself. Moses was human after all, and our experiences change our views on life and our expectations. He would have written those new rules with a different mindset. The first set of rules would have been written from a different level of awareness—that of God.

Second, from a human perspective, Moses had just witnessed a betrayal that overtook any understanding of compassionate thoughts. So Moses wrote the rules with a harsh hand to compensate for any wrongdoing. God didn't feel the betrayal; Moses did. In that act of being at one with God, he took on the responsibility of human behaviour. In that moment, he did not write from the word of God but from the thoughts of man; he was *thinking* about how to rule the people.

This resulted in the rules being relayed with an iron fist instead of compassion. The rule of responsibility for self-conduct wasn't actually covered as a way of choice for harmony; rather, it was covered as a choice for *disharmony* if not complied with. In other words, he ruled with punishment as the guideline rather than advocating for the peace of mind that come to those who complied. I understand this was written for those days, but from what we are told, the people had gone through a lot and didn't realize what they were doing; otherwise, they probably wouldn't have behaved in this way, according to my understanding.

It was not the *fault* of Moses. He would not have been consciously aware of that decision. But I also know that original guidelines on behavioural conduct were meant to apply to man but not woman. What we know as religion was intended to be a way for *men* to keep themselves in check. The rules that Moses presented included women and made the responsibility almost theirs to ensure the men remained pure. From a level of harmony with a balanced point of view, I can tell that these rules were written with a biased mind, not from a mind that had compassion as its mainstay, as is the mind of God.

These rules would have been interpreted as meaning that women were not included, but they took the brunt of these rules to help man achieve the desired state of blamelessness. Man has adapted the interpretation of these rules throughout history to keep us (women) at the forefront of their reason for failure. God has not been allowed to intervene, as Moses, who represented man, wrote these rules, and God made him the "link". Out of a given protocol of allowing the human race free will, this could not be altered. But it does go much deeper than this, and much further back in time.

Over the centuries that have gone by since then, we have adapted to a way of thinking that we are to blame—that it is all our fault. This is where a lot of it started, but whilst writing this I was urged to look into Abraham with the same eye. What I found there was equally astonishing. My findings would not go down well if I published them here, as they are so far reaching they would be too disturbing, and it would only be with a certain devoted mindset that the flaws could be acknowledged and seen as a spiritually scientific fact and not one of human failure.

But what I will say is that I can see and have acknowledged the fact that I have seen—thanks to the highest and greatest minds that have set me on this task of discovery to see what I could find in the ultimate truth of our spiritual heritage—the cause of our emotional uneasiness. We, as women, have been betrayed, but we have taken the betrayal as ours, though it had no right to be put on our shoulders. But we took it, so we paid the price; and we still do, as no one has given us any guidance that this is not right and that it needs to be corrected—apart from Jesus, that is; he tried his best.

You will find different versions of this story in varying concepts used to try to reach troubled minds. I write as it flows, and sometimes I double up on information when it fits into the time frame of my writing! Apologies, ladies, again. My intention is for you to make sense of the information I give you from different angles and levels of awareness, that you may know that whatever is going on in your life, *it's not your fault*. It was in the original delivery from the mind of man, not God. God has always been there for you in your own rite of purity in connection.

God believed that we would find our way to him, and I have. I had to find him from my own choice, and it was personal. Otherwise, you would not have seen the relevance or the connection that this has made to your life. You have been kept from knowing the biggest deception of all time. You have always had his respect for being female, with all that is expected of you as a bringer of life on earth.

The Universal Court of Law is your way of understanding the logic of your commitment and will serve you well through the feminine protocol frequency, which has been designed to allow you to receive wisdom in every situation. They will give you everything that you can give yourself as they communicate through your awareness of deeds done through intention and purpose. Emotional entanglement is the biggest flaw, so disentanglement is the main thing to look and aim for. We have been programmed to take the emotion of man, remember, and make it ours.

So back to my understanding of God being held prisoner. When you look at the biggest picture you are capable of, talking of it in layman's terms, Moses caused the problem by feeling bad for God. So God had to accept Moses's view, as he was representing God, that he was capable of this emotion. This emotion was disparaging, as God, in his total being of the frequency of compassion, is not capable of mind emotion.

Moses "grounded" God, making Him human in his thoughts with the human frailty of individual emotion by way of his thinking of how he would feel if he were God. God is God; he is not human, but he understands what we need to be more like him, ready to apply compassion when it is needed. So, to give you a brief explanation of this in a meaningful way, this is why you can always go to him with *any* problem. He doesn't judge, because he knows that when you are fully aware of the protocols of this emotion, you won't act like that. It would only be if you weren't aware, if you hadn't reached that level of comprehension, that you would think like that.

So when we slow down time yet again, we see that no intent was there to disrespect, and the rules on behaviour hadn't been written then. But once they were, the tribe of Moses hadn't received the rules yet—only Moses had. Moses had jumped the gun on his reactions. Again, it was *time* that was required to understand the fullness of this equation on his emotion, on behalf of God. He *assumed* God would be feeling those emotions. He did not know God as well as he could have; otherwise he would have been a bit smarter and fairer.

The result of his teaching, his misunderstanding as to the true nature of God, is what we are living today, and we are still taking the rap for the wrongdoing of man, as determined by Moses. Moses took every part of disrespect, dishonour, and immorality as his. He would have looked at it as the ultimate bad manners of humankind to treat God like this. But man could not be blamed for this going off the rails.

Man hadn't *felt* God's presence themselves; they only heard it spoken about. It wasn't their personal experience; they had to trust another human being for insight. That's what a leader does, but Moses wasn't God and could not reproduce the rules with the same eye as God. God would not have included women in those rules; he just wouldn't, as there was no need to. It was there for man to discipline their own desires, not for women to do that for them.

Our purity is the only thing that was necessary, and that is still the case. It was up to us to keep ourselves pure, and this was done by man keeping their mind disciplined, hence the need for rules. It was not up to us any more then than it is now. We are responsible for our own well-being and that of our children. Man is responsible for theirs. So where it went wrong was by making us, as women, responsible for the well-being of man by way of rules. We had taken on this responsibility out of love and compassion, freely out of our nurturing nature. But rules then made it our responsibility and expectation, turning it into a job rather than something given with our free will as an exchange for proper treatment deserving of our loving ways.

Our nurturing quality is a quality only we can understand fully as women, as it is imprinted in the memory of our spiritual DNA, linked to our emotion. So where it had been a natural quality of ours and we gave it as a free flow of energy from us to others, it was now expected of us. This was a totally different ball game, as it offered nothing in return that was truly important to our feminine state.

Religion, (man's way) does not require trust, understanding, or any of the codes of honour and respect that we need to function with harmony in our senses. It is expected of us to obey the rules and give unconditionally, whereas conditions are attached to the male mind and heart. We all know this is true, to some degree, for all of us. We have had to learn to disrespect ourselves, and we have always paid a price for that, as a sisterhood as well as in our own personal conduct towards ourselves.

Deep down, we always know better. Historically, we have just had to learn how to cut from our own personal communication that would have otherwise kept us within the realms of purity of intent. Man, through the wrong interpretation of Moses, has kept us in this state of low esteem and lesser soul worth for millennia.

It's always the same answer. The primary code of respect for the soul and for each other's needs and the natural rules that should apply is not being adhered to. Whether you are talking about Moses or a situation in your life now, no one wins at the end, apart from those amongst us that have made a really bad judgement call on their behaviour and conduct. These people know but don't care, and they use this soul abuse for their own personal desires, which do not include the well-being of humankind. And up until now, that could not be stopped. But now you know the real truth of our inherited demise. Either way, the change, the impact on the world, was and still is so far-reaching. It has played its part in creating a spiritual world war.

Now that I have your attention on this answer, there is an even deeper answer which links everything together with a clarity that I knew about but could not find the right link in conscious understanding to speak to you with an authority on—until now.

It is widely known and written in the Bible that at the inception of intelligent thinking, when Adam and Eve were created, God created what he believed would be the perfect mate for Adam in his duty as being the first of a new species and ready to procreate. Her name was Lilith, and she was given as an equal to man. But Adam did not want Lilith, as she did not want to conform to Adam's expectations of subservience, so he asked God to give him someone else that would be better suited to doing what she was told. Everyone knows this story. But let's look at this with fresh eyes regarding the ongoing consequences for woman. Lilith was *chosen* by God for Adam, as she had been created with the gifts of insight, intuition, and integrity—all that would be needed for a balanced, harmonious race to be created by human interaction with each other. Several understandings come out of this when we look deeper.

Man didn't want a strong woman in her own right. He didn't want to have to justify his actions by explanation or seek harmonious approval. He just wanted to have the say on how things were. He wanted the natural qualities that women have for his own use. He felt he had the right to use them on demand without explanation of the purpose for which he was using the many gifts that women have.

He treated it as arranged marriage with a clause that would allow him to opt out if he didn't like what he got. What we are also understanding with fresh eyes is that he was challenged by Lilith, who would not do as she was told. She was a true equal and would have had compassionate listening abilities, but Adam did not feel the need to explain his ways. He felt threatened by her intelligence.

Adam would not accept Lilith in her own right, so he asked for a more compliant model. Now look at history. Look at the women who were burnt at the stake. Look at Mary Magdalene, Joan of Arc, and Boudica; they are just a few of so many women misconstrued and stripped of their worth once it had served man's purpose. Women have never been allowed to gather momentum and collectively use their gifts in their own right for themselves. The disturbing fact is that every woman on this planet is being abused regarding her original birthright in some way. It's been allowed to continue because no one has gone through the right channels to put it right, because it wasn't known to us that this choice to challenge authority existed on a real basis that could change the world we live in. We have been given this opportunity now because I have challenged these things on a conscious level, and that complied with the rules.

I have had to prove with my purest of instincts just where it all went wrong and that this inequality is not only no longer acceptable but also needs to change before the human race destroys itself in the very way that Adam was allowed to just throw back Lilith because she didn't suit him, though God knew she was exactly what man needed to create harmonious living on earth. Lilith held the true link to the soul plane, where it is known what is needed to interact with one's soul and know one's true purpose. Eve did not have the strength to insist on compliant behaviour to ensure the morale code was adhered to. Adam did not know of this because, well, he didn't know. His mind was on a level of sexual submission apart from anything else. The rules on natural bonding because you feel respected, honoured and at one with the man you are going to give your virginity to are not important to a man. As such, we don't even see it like that anymore. Can you see how far away from our souls we have become, even on this subject? And the point is, ladies, this is where our true power lies. Even nature has the courtesy of giving the female a choice to see whether a male is sufficiently harmonious for all her needs as a mate. But I digress; more on that point later.

On that note, I believe we were an experiment to see whether man could uphold what he created and rule with harmony, as that is what he chose *against* the choice of God. He can't, and the experiment has failed; this much is obvious. On that note, I have brought the proof to the table of the governing body of universal law to give women a chance to show how it really should have been done in the first place.

Resetting the clock and the rules on a governing behavioural policy that is run by the moral code needs of the soul, is what should have been done and now, will be done. This will be overseen by God, and for the first time, goddesses will have a say too, as the truth of compassion and knowledge of application and of consequences need to be understood. How to achieve balance in this way needs to be explained and taught in a way that will make sense. This includes Lilith, who, for the sake of continuity of the story of our due inheritance, is named as a human who lived on earth for a short time and so had first-hand experience of what is now required to turn around this pathetic state that we call life and reclaim our true worth, as she brings her experiences to the table. This was the last piece in the puzzle I needed to find, so as to give her the right to speak for us and with us. Please note; all religions have their version of Lilith somewhere in their religious books, albeit it a deity. The point is, that it is time for the feminine strength of true place and higher purpose to be reassigned to all women, everywhere.

Many of those that sit in the Universal Court of Law have not lived a life on earth. They needed updating, and my role in this task was to help by using my soul and the emotion that went though it as the proof that was required, through my experiences. I have taken years to bring to them my personal experiences, which they were required to know, in the only reality that they can tune in to.

This is the only frequency that is true and cannot be bought in any way, as it sees all. It isn't what they were told; it is what they had to feel through my conscience and my conduct as I presented the truth to them. I had to keep pure in my approach to all things, including all experiences, as the link to my soul is too precious to let it be hoodwinked into believing a better way is possible without the need for this ruling code of conduct. I had to keep every one of you and your children in mind. I allowed all of this to happen when I could have just walked away on having found my own soul connection again. I came back for you, and this was the only way possible to ensure all the rules were complied with and there could be no loopholes. The Universal Court of Law and their authority on justice cannot be overruled, and they will ensure that we will succeed.

Just to confirm that last paragraph, although I talk of God quite a lot in my book, it is because it is man's version that has had the overriding say in our everyday lives. I know that the goddesses that have been helping women to try to overcome their male counterpart regarding the dominance of the mind through our hearts are now sitting amongst the Universal Court of Law, as they have to be part of the true nature of the feminine role. But as goddesses, they could not interfere. In fact, by giving relief to us, they have helped man still keep their hold on us because we hadn't found the way to bring it together. But this has given us time to resurface and a reason to keep going, which is what the soul is all about.

The intervention of goddesses has helped us, but as a metaphysical resource, they have had to remain separate. But we have had the help in coping, and we thank them for being there for us, although it must have broken their hearts to see us suffer. As a human, I have taken it all to court. In reality, there should not be a need for goddesses—or, for that matter, a god—to have to keep us healthy and happy. A moral code of conduct was always the first port of call, where disease and troubled minds do not survive in the soul level of purity.

The purest soul connection to your god or goddess can then be used for inspiration beyond that, which would enhance your life to a level you cannot imagine. Some of you may already be living in the world of the soul plane. Well done, you! This is then clarification for you and the realization of what you have achieved on your own.

More to the point, they needed to be heard to give us the opportunity in the future of mankind. A way forward has been thrashed out amongst the masculine and feminine counterparts to find a common primary code that will see balance for the future of the human race. There was no time left to apply any other form of justice, as, to be quite frank, it is the fault of no one who is alive today that we are in this miserable decline of humanity.

Before now, anyone could have taken his or her case to court and pleaded naivety by way of citing many cases in history which would have provided a get-out clause. A way for the most despicably evil amongst us and their possible clever interpretations of law had to be taken into account, so this had to be foolproof. A way had to be found to counteract any loopholes, and it has been.

A balance to take on board men and women has been found by bringing in a new constitution from the authority of the Universal Court of Law to uphold and preserve the purest nature of the soul of every living being. Any possible misdemeanours until now will be wiped clean, providing that now that this law is in place, we all individually abide by the ruling. This means that any transgressions you have carried out against another, or against yourself, will have an opportunity to have a line drawn under them, and it will be assumed that you did not know any better, as there has never been a *law* that made manipulation of any kind illegal. It was taken as a *given fact* that we all *knew* that to act dishonestly towards another soul was not honourable and would have to be dealt with when you crossed over to the soul plane (died), where everything would be made clear to you.

This new rule applies to every person, so anyone who does not sign up for it will also be under the new system but will be judged for their deeds and brought to justice in the soul whilst still living. This will not be pleasant for these people. The new law will be applied as soon as this book is published—as soon as its contents are made known. Natural law will be seen to work by those that see with fresh eyes.

This agreement has had to be made, as there is no time for leaving it until the "deathbed truth" now, as our well-being here on earth has become so disconnected from the truth of what should be happening here. It has been agreed that these steps need to be taken now if we are to maintain any decent level of free will that really matters. Our will has been used and abused since day one, on a conflict of interest, which I will explain as we go along.

My plea for intervention was heard, and it has taken twenty-five years for the proof of my findings to be taken to the point of acceptance. I cannot possibly explain *everything* that I found, so I have tried to make this as sensible as I can, that you may run with what I say, knowing the enormity of the task that lay before me all those years ago. I will just add here that this new way of thinking works; I am living proof of that.

I have followed the principle of what I was told would have to happen, and I agreed to this new ruling. I have also run a pilot scheme with clients of mine, and it has worked for them too. There is no reason that this primary code of the soul cannot work for anyone who has his or her heart in the right place. It has been designed to protect the vulnerable on every level, so as to keep the sanctity of the soul plane intact.

It cannot be manipulated or bought at any price, as all souls are laid bare for the all-seeing eye of the Universal Court of Law and the souls that they represent and protect. That means you, your children, your loved ones, and those you have yet to meet. Nothing escapes this authority on the justice of souls and the injustices of the past—especially those things regarding women and children,.

From the minute you consciously subscribe to this new way (as set out later on in the book), you are acknowledging you have signed up to be included in this protection of the soul. There is no need for you to physically acknowledge this to me; you just need to know for yourself. I am just the one that has made this possible for you to do. If, however, you want to be a conscious part of the allegiance of women worldwide, there is a way to do so given to you further on in this book to ensure your voice will be heard.

It would be great for you to spread the word or let me know if you are on board with this new commitment and determination to succeed that is required. It is no more than that, but some will find it easier than others. I am here for any of you that need guidance and further explanation, but it is a new way, and your acceptance to yourself needs to be loud and strong so your soul knows you will work towards changing the world you live in, and by "work" here I mean your everyday living and behaviour through your actions and reactions. It cannot work if you are not applying the code of conduct to yourself, because that's where your responsibility lies.

That's why it is so important for you to acknowledge the spiritual law agreement and code of conduct further on in this book. The law cannot get involved with your feminine role unless you support its presence amongst the Court of Universal Appeal. The court will insist on a code of conduct *towards* women that we have agreed to and will adhere to.

We are asking for no more and no less than what we have afforded man, so we cannot lose this fight for the right of our souls to be heard. But this includes playing your part in invoking your true worth as a female and the right for protection, as you would not expect any form of abuse from a man or, indeed, another woman. There is only one way this can succeed, and humility plays a big part. Don't worry! All will be explained.

You cannot fail in this, because you are a woman; I have already paved a way for you to succeed. The more you grow in wisdom as your natural instincts evolve to the level they should be at, the more you will see how the law is working for you through the feminine protocol. You will experience a new sense of well-being as you let go of the condition of the past which has ruled our lives because of the choice Adam made at the inception of life for this new human race. And this is why: Man has never needed to look at himself as deeply as women can, because Adam deemed it not necessary to be done. He didn't know about taking responsibility for his actions. He just wanted to happen what he wanted to happen. (The words "brat" and "spoiled" come to mind.) God complied with Adam's wishes because Adam was created, and he took the word of Adam that he knew what he was doing, because that was God's deal with man. God has been the one to slowly lose his authority on our soul-searching need for his protection as his daughters, because man wanted a say in when intervention was required. In hindsight (and we have had plenty of time for that), where did the original fault lie here?

Intervention from God was only ever allowed (so it seems) when support was needed to keep a woman standing by her man no matter what she suffered under his rule. Hence, this is why man rules religion and always has. As no one has been able to bring our mistrust to court before now, this situation has been allowed to continue.

I have had to tune in on a certain frequency, where the individual laws upheld by religion had no hold on me and I could not be stopped from reaching the court of universal law, and being in the presence of God. I had been heard and proof was required to uphold my claim. Believe me, I have been to hell and back to lead you all out of the subservient life that we all lead in one way or another without us realizing it, as our compassionate, empathic hearts are taken for granted at best, manipulated at worst.

On the subtlest of levels, you are not in control of your full worth as far as your feminine protocols are concerned. We have, in many cases, exchanged them for a worth that keeps us in denial through forced choice. There are many levels that can be discussed here, but as always, I have tried to give you the real truth of us on a level that you will be able to comprehend. We have a chance now to put the human race into a state of harmony in the long run by all of us being given the strength of Lilith, who was denied her place in the beginning.

I don't say it will be easy to undo the many misconceptions that have led us to be so lacking in worth as we are now, with so little regard for the innocence and purity of the minds of our children. We have to stand up and be counted for who we all are, students of Lilith, who has a strong ability for intelligent, emotional integrity. This is the feminine protocol. This is grounding our natural instincts in our own lives on an everyday basis and making them count.

We will need compassion for ourselves first, not pity or sympathy, to go forward to gain compassion for others. Each one of us has her own journey to make in her own world; that is the story of us. Looking with fresh, new eyes will help you to succeed in finding that ability in you that has always been there but has been hidden from you by our society and what it expects of us now as women.

Enough said about the complexities of the past from this level of interpretation. You will find your own way of interpreting this truth on a level that will further increase your own awareness of your true inheritance. Putting this information to one side for now, as it is rather mind blowing, I will continue with other understandings that relate to religious states, as what I have just told you was a state of humanity before religion was invented, although it was written in the Bible in a different way.

2

OPENING UP TO THE SECRET KNOWLEDGE OF THE SOUL

I will write more about the metaphysical timeline of my journey now to continue with my story. I will also write of my further understandings on my spiritually scientific route with other explanations and proofs of my metaphysical findings.

There have been many areas that I have been given to research that have shown me how the demise of our humanity has come about. It was the piecing it all together that finally made it all worthwhile.

I have travelled to many places, again instinctively and intuitively (using the language of the fifth dimension, the soul frequency), and I found truths that would remain unseen (as a more detailed timeline of events to follow). I could feel pockets of energy left there from bygone ages, waiting to be tapped into and uncovered by anyone who cared to look for the sake of humanity. It felt that they were waiting for *me* to take it to the realms of universal law for scrutiny and deliberation.

I must add at this point that I am in total awe of this fact. I am grateful and feel very honoured that I was the one chosen in this way to help the cries of injustice be brought to the *only* justice system that *cannot* be overridden. As I look back whilst writing this, I am seeing a snapshot of the journey I have undertaken, and I remember that it started out as a knowing, a feeling that something just wasn't right, as I have said previously. And this was just to do with my own life, initially.

This made me immediately think of other women—that the same thing is happening to us all. It has led to me understanding pretty much everything I would ever need to know about anybody or anything, to be able to guide through the thorns of life. I have been supported by a world beyond this, and I understand it and acknowledge my gratitude on a daily basis.

They have had to have equal trust in me as I have in them. This is the only way this *could* work. No stone has been left unturned. If it has, my trust is that it wasn't meant for me to find what was under it; it was not part of my mission to do so at that time.

In 2003 I was visited by one of my guides from another level, who "blueprinted" over a trusted friend as we discussed my latest findings. His face turned into a white skeletal frame as we spoke, but not like one I would recognize as being that of someone from this world. It felt ancient. He said to me, "What you are is a spiritual anthropologist." It was such a revelation for him to put into words what I am. It also aptly describes exactly what I do. I had never heard of that term and was asked to write about this in a local spiritual magazine shortly after this happened. They had never heard of the term either -and I was asked to explain what it meant. I see now on the Internet that it is a term used commonly than I imagined.

My many, many years of research into the depths of consciousness that are there for us has proved time and time again that my version of the truth is far more believable than you might think. My version of God with the aid of universal law has healed many people and given them a new lease on life. I show them that they were not able to see the original cause of the problem, and I explain how I came to that conclusion by making sense of their words to me when describing their plight as seen in the real truth of soul law.

I decipher the real message their soul has been trying to convey to them. It then releases the trauma, allowing them to be freed of the subconscious hold over them. They get to understand a different logic that makes sense to their troubled minds. This all happens in one session, with no need for follow-up or continual counselling. The problem is dealt with there and then.

It is up to individuals to engage in continual learning of the format, with a new attitude, a different viewpoint, and a new approach to life. To explain a little further, when other problems surface, there is already a guideline in place—a new, revised blueprint in the mind on how to approach would-be trauma and emotional blockages.

One session with the frequency that I access is all that is needed. The person then takes responsibility for his or her own learning, therefore taking dependency on others out of his or her story. A strict diet of a new set of rules to live life by is given to the person, and a copy of those rules is within this book. It is a requirement that he or she uphold the truth of his or her own soul, but this is given at the point of consultation to avoid conflicting stories of other truths getting in the way.

Just to be clear, this frequency has nothing to do with religion. It has to do with the fact that you are human. Man created religion. If you believe in God, I remind you that he is now, and always was, there for you simply because you are human. I have reconnected many by re-educating their minds to hear the messages of their souls so they can interact with their god themselves. I have positive proof that it is within my power to achieve this, so I am attempting to do this en masse, as time is running out for the majority of us, who are *very* disconnected. It will be too much of a struggle for re-education to be possible; hence the need for a universally accepted code of conduct to re-establish control of the senses—the way it should always have been.

Let's have a look at how religion came about. Please forgive the simplicity of how I have written this. It has been written in this way *only* to give an overview of the general understanding of religion and its truth and origin so it can tick a box in that logical side of your mind that does not require emotion to find answers.

This is a different approach than the one that I have written before, and there are so many approaches to the same subject that I continually try to find new ways to relay the logic of my findings to inspire change in your life by giving you this new truth. Although we now have an understanding of Lilith's place in all of this, I have written what is to follow as stepping stones for you to identify with your logic, from that most powerful knowledge, and relate through the channels of your mind. This is so you can join the dots of understanding the sisters of the past who had no known choice of their own to make. I have also taken into account that this is ultimately about *you* and your journey, so I have gone over the subject of religion in different ways, as religion affects most of our lives to some degree.

I believe we all agree that man owned the hand that created religion and believed this was what was required to be done, along with the idea that we are to obey man as God's envoy.

In my opinion, as you already know, I believe that religion was for *man* to educate *man* on his conduct. Woman did not need to be ruled by this discipline. We were born to nurture and look after the spiritual well-being of all; therefore, the rules given to man were for themselves. Women pass down the wisdoms of our gender, daughter to daughter. The wisest of men would have been well nurtured as sons by their mothers or mother figures.

The religious law became the total meaning of how to behave, and woman was supposed to treat man as though he represented God. We were taught to be grateful for man, we were taught not to question the word of man. We trusted—we had to trust—that this was what God wanted from us. We were taught right from the beginning of intelligent life that God was an all-seeing eye that expected women to bow down to the hand of man, as the hand of man represented God.

Is it any wonder that women stay in abusive relationships, blaming themselves for being the reason for men's anger and feeling that they are responsible for the cause of this and it is therefore their responsibility to carry the burden of the man's behaviour towards them? Nothing has really changed, has it? And it all started because of a religious misinterpretation, whether by intention or by naivety regarding the fact that it was only man that religion was created for.

A woman didn't, and still doesn't, need the sort of discipline a man needs. Her needs are different and do not involve the same strategy that a man needs for control. But man has made it our responsibility in a way that keeps them free from blame. But do you see how, for millennia, our trust, on a very basic level, has put man above woman, ensuring that we feel responsible for their well-being, their state of mind?

The sad fact of the matter is that on a core level of understanding, this is actually true. But we are always meant to do it on an *equal* level of respect. It is the honouring of us by our men that we instinctively *want* to nurture their needs. A woman does this so that a man is proud of the attention a mother gives to the children, not jealous; so that the family home rests in the arms of his wife or the mother of his children; and so she can still feel the power of also being the mistress, using all of her charms when the children are not around.

A woman does all of this with an energy that is all-encompassing love. She gets this from feeling loved herself. She does so knowing that *her god*, her connection, is above anything that man can offer. And it has to stay that way. Her husband does not *replace* her god; her husband is the manifestation of her god to provide her physical needs on earth so she can fulfil her role as being pivotal in family life, as far as *well-being* is concerned. One must remember that she is the one with the ultimate connection of true guidance and the ability to know the path of wisdom.

There has been a massive entanglement of emotion, which has been the destroyer of happiness for most of us. This has come in the form of misunderstandings, misalignments of truth, and a communication level that doesn't know how to convey feelings on a responsive level that harms no one.

It has been bred into many nations that the rules on living as written in the Bible are what God wanted to be conveyed, as written by the hand of man. This is far from the truth. But from my own first-hand experience, I know that God is gentle, kind, and respectful, and that he is an all-encompassing *father* to all women—one who will protect woman above all. If we take this further (and this has been proven to be true in my own life), if any man disrespects or dishonours a woman, he will have God to deal with.

I never saw it at the time, but hindsight has shown me this truth. It was so obvious to see, but I wasn't looking for myself. I have always felt a knowing that I am protected—always. I have gained enough strength from the situations in my own life to absolutely, categorically say to you now that this is a truth that is undisputed in my own experiences and remains unchallenged.

I have witnessed the demise of men in my life who have disrespected their role and not recognized the protection of God (the father), who reigns supreme in the world of a moral code. They were not being observed as the priority of all commands for a man over himself. I say nothing because the consequences of dishonour are nothing to do with me. It is down to man and his soul conscience to intervene with a disciplined response when faced with looking at themselves in the mirror of truth.

This statement is not fiction. This is how it has been from my own personal experiences throughout my life, but consciously for the last twenty-five years, the Universal Court of Law has assisted me. I will not go into detail here, because those people have already been dealt with by God's hand. It is not up to me to further persecute them for any wrongdoing towards me; if I were to do so, I would be no better than those that continued to persecute me, as described elsewhere in this book.

The unfortunate twist on the general understanding of most people is that our earthbound souls have accepted man's version of truth as to what we have *chosen* to be the case. But we were not given a choice. We were *told* this is how it was, and we believed this to be true because there were no other options being given. We have never questioned this on the deepest levels. We question only our unspoken unhappiness.

I do not think that this was a deliberate viewpoint of control, but I do believe it was the ego of the day that created the diversity in common understandings of creative thought, and it became biased because *time* became the quality that was required for instruction, and *time* was called on by man before it understood the vastness of the decisions that were being made.

There are no *automatic* protocols in place at present, to ensure that a true moral code on soul equality and behaviour has been instilled on a very basic level of comprehension, from my observations. Man has always believed, according to my investigations, that the original first writings on religion still holds the say on who we are meant to be. Man was, in my opinion, doomed from the very first thought on this.

But women have paid the consequences of the original misinterpretation of role acceptance. There is, once again, so much evidence to support what I say. You need only look at what is written for us to be guided by, right from the inception of Adam and Eve and what we are supposed to take from that story. I will not go into that again here.

I write a lot with regard to Christianity, because that is what my school day teachings were all about. I have looked into just about every religious teaching at its source, independently. I believe in a universal law which sees all, and I have been allowed the privilege of a unique frequency that will ensure that no deviance of the law can be bought for the sake of an individual's whims that do not have the universal conscience of spiritual well-being and harmony as their uppermost intention.

This frequency has never failed to support and nurture my needs. It has also continued to allow me to help others find a way when all other avenues were not strong enough to support their devasted souls in moving away from a road that sees only depression and contemplative suicide as the only option.

That is the role of universal law—to make sure *all facts are made known*. God is outside of the law in a *certain respect*, but he resides in a space provided by one's own soul, so in fact, he is the central point of *deliverance* of law through compassion at the soul level. The same attitude is afforded a judge and jury here on earth, but here it relates to the physical incarnation. God allows compassion to intervene until enough time has naturally passed to bring situations into a state of play where they can be seen for what they are and be dealt with. But time is now the issue, as I have mentioned elsewhere in this book.

The world of universal justice cannot wait for mankind to see the light of its original choices by being hasty in dismissing Lilith without realizing the consequences; it's just not going to happen. So that, as I have come to understand through my own journey, is the reason I have been given the support to bring this to light now, because I wouldn't accept a truth that didn't sit right with my subconscious-to-conscious connection within my own mind.

Man is having to pay the price for the injustice that has been served on woman by allowing a change of management at the top of the chain. Religion no longer has the controlling angle on God. Universal law is now in charge, and God is in his correct place as the almighty father of women, first and foremost to ensure we get a fair deal, as is his loving duty. As I mentioned earlier, all goddesses are now part of this new path, that we may ensure all points of domination by man are a thing of the past. The energy that man was and is using will be allowed to bring us to the fore by default, as the natural leaders for well-being and harmony, by way of the primary code of conduct that the soul plane adheres to out of choice.

Maybe, in the grand scheme of things, this is the only way this would work in our favour. Man's power over the mind is a strong quality that has no place for harmonious living by true equality, and that would probably never be accepted by man. He was given the opportunity to show he could do the job first, by his own choice. Now that this has been proved ineffectual—and I do stress here that this is the case as far as well-being for all is concerned—it is now our turn to prove our worth as leaders in a world that has not known how to use the compassion that we are capable of in the right way.

For whatever reason, it is my path to ensure this can now be the case for all humans that do not feel that justice is commonplace in their lives. I am bringing it into the *now* so a new path can be laid where a new balance of emotional integrity provides fresh insight into situations that happen in your life, providing you with support for positive outcomes.

The basic *understanding* of a moral code of conduct was all that was needed. But religion has expanded upon it and made it difficult to understand, keeping religion in control of our well-being and soul connection to the Almighty. No one has really come up with a simple-to-understand moralistic code of behaviour that really can be universally understood, knowing that responsibility starts and ends with our own actions. This I am dealing with, and a simple-to-understand written code of conduct is given further on.

As I make clear, I have assisted just as many men with troubled minds as I have women. But as a woman, I know women best. Women teach women so we can then pass on our teaching, but does not make me biased in any way regarding the people I help, of which some cases are detailed elsewhere in this book.

I will leave that line of thought there for the moment, as this is a subject that is far reaching in its understanding at this level of comprehension and this book is not about blame. It is about identifying cause and effect. It is about seeing what hasn't worked and reworking what we have learnt to the best of our abilities for a better future.

This is the intelligent understanding of what has been the story of us until now. Now you can have a choice on what you decide to be the story of you. This is where all my research, my findings, and my journey have led me to. I am now going to change the level of description on my presentation of facts. I ask you to open your mind to keep pace with what I have to say.

3

EXPLANATIONS FROM ANOTHER PERSPECTIVE

If you are ready for this new understanding, it will intrigue you. The difficulty I have already understood whilst writing this is that there are many different levels that interact constantly, but when writing, one can write about them only one at a time.

My research has overlapped, has had bits missing, and I have had to go back into research mode many times as a certain piece of information reaches me but doesn't make total sense the way it is presented at first. But when I step back and look at the bigger picture, I can see where it fits in. Determination, persistence, humility, and stubbornness are qualities that have got me through the doubts and fears that are ever present in this world, and this is worth remembering, as this could happen to you too. I pushed ahead so I could give you answers to pull you out of apathy.

We are all sisters, mothers, aunts, and cousins in this quest, and respect and honour will be afforded to you from all of those that have gone before and died trying to make sense of their lives through understanding built on lies. It is the *implementation* of the information that I give you that will make the difference to you.

The main point is that we don't need to fight on this new level of interpretation that the route of the fifth dimension, the level of interpreting instinct and intuition, has to offer. I have attempted to bring to you a synopsis of my research that has led me to the understanding that a new regime of human behaviours and guidelines are necessary to bring back the connection between the God that is there for you as an independent entity and as a Father whom you can trust implicitly, who would never see harm come to you.

For those that cannot see their way forward into thinking about God being this loving father figure because of shattering experiences with their own fathers, believe in the authority of universal law that sees all. Believing in God is *not a requirement* to shattered souls; it is not your fault if you cannot find it in your heart to believe in God. A lot of people do believe in a God, and it is the reputation of the God that is truly there for you that wishes to be seen and understood that your human experience may be one of happiness, not heartache. This is all down to interpretation of the facts regarding what is happening to you.

Emotional integrity sees that it has become against our nature to use our natural gifts in the way that was *originally* imprinted into us in our spiritual DNA (yes, there is such a thing). It has been bred out of us to question things that do not sit well with us on those deeper levels. Someone needed to stand up and refuse to be put off by current thinking regarding our status and the way it is meant to be for us.

We have been led to believe that it is we who have a problem with our understanding. In a worst-case scenario, this leaves your conduct unstructured and at odds with society, as it makes your presence uncomfortable to be around. You become detached, even from your own understanding, as your loneliness at not being heard takes hold of "sensible" reasoning.

It then progresses to a way that makes you at fault for being misunderstood, but there are no immediate guidelines and no immediate teaching provided for you to challenge what you feel is wrong. You wouldn't know where to start.

This new level of communication will take you back to your original imprint, which you feel is there, though you cannot understand what it is you are feeling. Put another way, do you suffer from depression? Have you had thoughts of committing suicide because you don't fit in or no one understands you? Have you got a drug or alcohol habit? Do you allow yourself to be abused because that's what happens to you? Have you no self-worth, always feeling "less than"? Do you feel alone, scared to speak up because you might be humiliated, mocked, or deprived of friends if you don't act in a certain way? This is your proof that you feel the connection—the strand of spiritual DNA that we have been born with. What you do not understand is how to use it properly—how to interpret what your intuition, your connection, is really telling you. And do you know what? You are closer to hearing its truth than those who live "normal" lives. Because you are different, not like "normal" people, others see *you* as having the problem, and you accept this as your truth. But you are feeling the distress of the universal soul and taking it on board as though it is your problem.

You have had no way of knowing this. You can't identify it because you don't know how to access the frequency, the thought pattern, that would make your messages come to you in a comprehensible way for your senses to pick up. There is no proper guidance. Correction: there *hasn't* been any guidance until now. So the flow of information you call upon just continues to be received through the distortion of truth, being misunderstood and misinterpreted regarding its true worth.

Your personal connection to your soul, and the wisdom of all souls, remains hidden from your requirements because you never call upon its wisdom and guidance. You have never been allowed to know of its existence, because no one knows the teaching of how to access this level of awareness.

With perhaps a simpler understanding, you could relate to it as being like trying to tune in to a particular radio station. In this case, the signal is too weak because of interference, so you pick up another, more local, one—one on which you can hear clearly what is being broadcast—and you listen to that instead. It is more convenient. The cycle never gets broken.

If, like me, you have always been surfing for the right answer, looking for a clue that might be on the level you are on, stop for a moment and consider whether this is what you are missing? Is this the inspiration that you have been searching for without knowing it?

I hope you will recognize that the truth of what I say is real and it hits a nerve somewhere within your mind.

But trust me; earlier on in my journey, I spent thousands of pounds on following false clues in the hope of finding someone, anyone, or an organization that thought like me and that I could link with and share experiences with on the level I could see things on. Nope.

I thought that I could further my teachings and feel accepted in a world that is outside of the normal, uneventful life that I was imploding in. The answer was never there from others; it was my own connection that I already had that saw me through, and continues to see me through, every trauma, every grey area, and every torment. Once I had accepted that fact, everything settled down and I was put through my training to make me the leader I need to be for you all.

You see, after twenty-five years of continual study, I realized I was only proving to myself that no one I had met had the connection of understanding life and how to deal with adversity as much as I had already been given it. I had learned how to keep balance and harmony intact, to know my starting point, and to return to that at all times to resolve the daily life issues that I have to face in this world, where lies are better things to believe in than truths. (As I said elsewhere, the alternative is so much more convenient and less of a hassle.)

So it was all a reverse understanding for my point of view. I am sure the masters that are my mentors just stood back watching, saying, "Here she goes again. I wonder how long it will take her this time to realize the inevitable."

I know what my quest is: to re-educate the senses of woman so she, in turn, can re-educate the senses of man. This is the *only* way this can work. Women must teach and guide women first, and then we can teach our children through harmonic understanding— another term for wisdom. That is our natural, feminine way to be. Any other way is not true to our nature.

If we try to demand, this will not work as harmony. It will become harmful and judgemental. That is the masculine, patriarchal approach. Be harsh in teaching another and you will be judged with the same harshness. Be soft, natural, and caring, teaching *why* things have to be done in a certain way, and your patience will be rewarded with confident children and loving relationships.

The children need new guidelines, and the mother is ultimately responsible for this. All children are the responsibility of the mother to guide in spiritual well-being and nurturing codes. The father is there to provide for the mother and his children and to protect them from harm, so as to allow this teaching to be fulfilled. The wife also nurtures the husband in ways that only she can.

There are as many ways as there are ideas on nurturing. But the husband will respond with tenderness, loving, and oneness with his wife in this new level of understanding. They share a life together that can grow only in happiness, as the wisdom of the woman is always there to guide and interpret dramas that occur and traumas that invade harmony. The husband trusts his wife's guidance.

How did that statement sit with you?

How far from the truth of today's standards of living does that truth feel to you?

Welcome to the fifth dimension of interaction. It's an awareness of personal emotional control that you will experience as you understand that feeling of *freedom* that is present as you learn that you are not responsible for others' emotions. As you do this, you will feel strength and knowing regarding your choices of when to speak and when not to.

This frequency and the rules set by universal law (as explained further on in this book) allow you to be *you* without being judged, as under these rules you judge yourself and then upgrade your thinking, naturally. It offers time out so you can find answers to your insecurities and questions. Clues appear that can help you on your way.

The connection of others to harmony is *theirs*; they have to find it. It is not up to you to do that for them and carry them. You can show them the way, but you cannot insist they learn. Again, that's up to them. Learning how to discipline *your* mind not to take on board others' controlling ways that have not evolved into taking responsibility for *their* own actions is just as important as learning how to take on board your own actions towards others.

It's all a new way of learning how to achieve disentanglement of emotion, which is rife in, and at the heart of, any disharmony in relationships, and at the heart of most illnesses and diseases. It's the entanglement that has caused the problem. This goes back to the original cause, which I spoke of earlier. Man believed that he was in control of woman's emotion because he said so, and we did as we were told. So we have continued to believe we are responsible for his emotion, which isn't ours. But we take it on board as though we need to protect man from pain by making it our own. This is what we do; this is what we have been taught to do. It has been instilled into us by a law that we believe tells us what man deserves to get from us.

This is yet another understanding of what the fifth dimension of understanding can teach you. It is there for us to set the record straight. We can see what went wrong, and we are being given an opportunity to put it right. We have to dig deep, but we will be given help with this.

I repeat this for those of you that feel that this teaching could pull you away from your god. It won't; it can't. It is God that allowed me to write this, and it will only enhance your ability to be compassionate towards yourself and others. If your instincts are to believe in your God, he is waiting for you to find him too—and I will show you the route, the way, of how to do this so you can talk to him with an increased level of perception.

If you do not believe in a god but believe in natural law, this is where universal law resides too. Once you have understood and agree with the simple guidelines put forth later in this book, all levels of understanding the true qualities of being human are opened up to you without any religion being involved.

This practice is the true forerunner of religion. Religion can run alongside this simple moral code, or you can just use these simple guidelines to live your life by. There is true freedom to learn once you have assimilated the fifth dimension into your life and are committed to it. It will give to you the same commitment and devotion you can give to it, so you will always be in control of your teachings. This teaching uses your life as the "book" you can turn to once you have understood how to search for clues relating to your life.

I have tried to start all of this off with what has happened to me, in order to show you how to look for the points in your own life that have been the trigger points of discovery for you now, as you begin to understand an alternative way of looking for the wisdom that lies within your own personal experiences.

Because it is only you that knows you best, your memories provide all the clues you need to be successful in your journey of life, and no one else needs to know of your findings—unless you wish to share them physically with others. As you find the hidden answers, new truths will come out. You can then reassess your actions and understand why you reacted the way you did in any previous encounter with adverse drama in your life.

Your past conduct was carried out through uncensored thoughts. You may begin to realize many things about yourself and those you care for. I have been given my own reign on how to teach this, to make sure it is kept in the hands of women this time to bring about this upgraded form of spiritual teaching. Jesus tried to fight in our corner, as you know, but we all know how that ended up for him.

There are many things that I can tell you that I have found in my studies, both in this realm and the realms of those that have come before us; I have found hidden truths that were not talked about in the way they actually happened.

There is evidence—once again, in plain sight—to exonerate Judas, for example. Also, Jesus knew his work could not be stopped, for he had universal law on his side. For once a human being has tried to interact with those in power, on whatever level that is, to show that incorrect teaching is not being corrected, that the advice being given is not being heeded, his *intention* cannot be stopped but can only be delayed. He knew this when he was on the cross. He had achieved what he needed to on the level of persistence and commitment. He did not stop; he was stopped by man. That makes universal law—the natural law of truth, the code of the soul—a work in progress.

Those that have no knowledge of universal law and the true power that it holds have no idea whom they are messing with. Time has no bounds in this frequency, and it will be heard eventually. Short-sightedness of this fact is what has caused the downfalls of the biggest and most troublesome characters that have lived, and some that still live on this earth. It is only their own souls that they will have to face. But their souls are part of the universal soul that sees all. There is no escaping this fact.

I have made it my business to find out all of this information so I can allow you to know truth will always, in all ways, be seen. Naivety is no longer an option once this book has been published and is amongst the population for all to see. I have heard the call of the soul plane to bring this to you and have spent my whole life in preparation for this. I know it is now the chance of women everywhere to hear the call in their hearts to ensure they do their bit towards bringing an awareness into this world that has been lacking since time began. We start with ourselves, our own lives, and spread the word on how we did it.

Think of Joan of Arc (she just sprang to mind) and all women that knew what I now know and used their sight to try to help man succeed in his challenges. They were duped as well, and women everywhere were killed for using their sight. It's so obvious that man is *scared* of the power we hold, but this is only because of the misconception of the original guidelines having missed a valuable point of emotional integrity. But is it any wonder he has kept us from it by controlling our trust, our good nature, and our loving hearts?

It is man's fear that stops him seeing the truth of who we are. We have taken his fear on board and made it ours, giving him the power which he truly does not know how to use where harmony is concerned. Man has not been designed to do this; he does not have direct access to the frequency that is required. He knows of it and thinks that he is truly connected to it, but he cannot access it because of his gender.

We have lost our way through being denied our true nature. The twist is that we did it *willingly* as far as the rules that govern

43

our existence, as a matter of law. And those that are in privileged positions that run this world know this fact. As no one has bought our case to court, this has continued throughout the existence of religion, and to date—until I turned up, that is, and I say this with no ego: it was for *justice* that I started out on my quest, nothing more. Something inside—a burning pain—would not let me stop searching, researching, and pushing even further until I was heard.

I do this for *all* women, everywhere. It is of no consequence what your colour, creed, or religious beliefs have made you believe your worth is. There are no bounds or authority on my findings or my intention to put an end to the terrible plight that most women are having to endure in some shape or form. It is now there for all women to be able to hear this call and join our kindred sisterhood, who will put the existence of our children first and will fight for a justice in a way that has never been done quite like this.

It will take courage and determination, and this I can help you with.

It has taken many, many years for the chance to surface again for someone to find the absolute truth of how the will of women has been abducted to keep those in power that truly have the say on how this world is conducted, and to what end. I am not particularly talking of religion here. I am talking of how money and emotion run this world—and, above all, fear: fear that we are not seen as good citizens, fear of illness, fear of death, and fear of life.

This keeps those in present power there, in a safety net over an ever-decreasing circle of life for the rest of us.

Everything I write is intended to give you knowledge and a sense of proportion as to the scale of things, but most of all, it is intended to give you inspiration to take your life seriously, for your own sake and for the sakes of your children. Further on in the book, I will detail simple guidelines and talk of some of the ways that this teaching, this frequency that I am reminding you how to connect to, has helped those willing to hear to start on a new path.

I am giving you everything I possibly can to help you cut through your present acceptance of who you are, whom you give your energy to, and who takes it as a given right for them so to do. Your children are the only ones that really matter. They deserve to be given a chance of *true* freedom. But it has to be done in the way of soul pain release, which has never been done before.

For them to learn the guidelines, you, as their mother, need to be able to teach them. So let's be brave and lead them into a world where fear has no hold on outcome, because there you can teach them the correct new way to think and feel and behave.

Please forgive me if it feels as though I am not sticking to the point of really getting in there and telling you what "it"—this new way of thinking—entails. I am explaining different mentalities, different aspects, of how we all got to this point of preferring lies to truths, and how easy it would be to just let this be just another book to read as something out of the ordinary.

I have taken an oath on your behalf to do whatever I can to raise your awareness to a level that will allow you to hear the sorrow and the happiness that all our ancestors are feeling, as they, too, were denied a truth of life whilst still incarnate. Their sorrow is a result of their not having known the truth until they passed from this earthly existence. Their happiness has come about in their knowing that you are being given an opportunity to know *now* that all the time there is life, and there is time to change your outlook and the future.

I am now going to "bring this down to earth" and talk about my own journey, to give you another aspect of my findings and the proof that I was searching for.

I go back to 1998 and pick up my story from there.

Over the next few years, my knowledge grew, but I never revisited the room where I had been so happy speaking personally, on a one-on-one basis, with the Almighty. Instead I felt the presence of different "masters" who knew much of the world but at the same time wanted to learn reciprocally through my experiences of what this world was like now. I knew that I was doing all of this for women, from a woman's point of view. I felt that I was to bring something into the world that should be here but isn't.

I have had to find my own path and make it my own journey to ensure I abide by the laws of a universal code that I trust implicitly. One must do so if one is to prove the point that such a law exists. It has been lowered by other realms of the mind, where humankind wants to quicken the pace by "cheating", desiring an outcome of events that they are not going to trust to luck or judgement by natural law.

This is where the ancient laws of Egyptian understanding made so much sense to me. Basically, your heart is weighed against a feather at the point of death. This is all about a soul code of living. That was just the way it was in those ancient days. Even then this was the case until corruption set in. Those who had money and position bought their way out of indiscretions and wrongdoing via bribes to the high priests, who said they would create a way so these people would be "overlooked" at the point of judgement.

I was guided to look into this original form of law based on morality. This is the oldest written law that I have been able to find, and it makes total sense. The original intention and purpose of this law is what my findings have concluded to be parallel to the unique justice system that exists in the fifth dimension. From my conclusion, what the high priests were doing was using reasoning in an adverse way, treating it as a truth that had credence to absolve conscious wrongdoing, though the original purpose of this clause was for naivety due to misunderstanding or misinterpretation of facts.

I do understand this law in the greatest of detail, but it does not need to be explained here. You can follow my thoughts on that if it interests you. What I have stated here is my interpretation of *how* it was used. The books available for general use just state that shabti dolls were used to pay the way for miscreant conduct that went against the laws that were present on behaviour towards others in whatever form, direct or indirect. I have sought wisdom through the fifth dimension to find a deeper truth of how this was supposed to work, to allow some insight of the beginning of soul abuse. All of this involves money and power as an instigator to have real truth swept under the carpet. Once again, universal law cannot be fooled. I have found this out as a truth that was hidden from view. This was a blatant misuse of trust. Now look at your own life for a second. The law trusts that you are truthful in your judgements.

Have you given your trust to others that have abused your trust? Or have you abused the trust someone gave to you meaningfully, to reach a goal that put you above that person in some way, without considering the consequences? There really is a fine line. This teaching will show you how to correct your thinking and make you more aware.

I continue to share my journey with you. Even now, as I open up to you, continuous wisdoms are being given to me, entering my mind as higher truth and various examples on cause and effect to share with you all. So once again, if my writing is spasmodic in its teaching, apologies.

But it is true that my writing flows, and I can never recreate a passage once it has left my fingertips. If I try to write notes to put down later, it all gets revised and upgraded as I write. Such is the working of the flow of universal energy on this subject, so dear to the hearts of those guiding my every move on this. It is known just how long it has been since some fresh air was blown into this subject and the truth behind it finally brought to the attention of us all.

The soul plane and all its inhabitants have waited patiently for me to get myself up to speed with what I felt was important to relay to you in the way it needed relaying.

I had also been given to understand that if I continued to learn and keep my faith and commitment true to my cause, I would be allowed to be the spokesperson for women. I needed far more training, but on a conscious, equal basis now. I have also been taught true magic on my journey and came to understand the hold of voodoo and black magic in the eyes of those that revere these forms of superior power and find them to be all-encompassing.

Respecting and honouring any form of soul deliverance is something that teaches wisdom to be the guide, through intention and purpose. I am truly grateful for the knowing I have received whilst looking into these forms of spiritual guidance.

I received wisdoms in exchange for personal experiences that I allowed myself to enter into so the true nature of treatment could be seen and be felt by the frequency dealing with the law of the fifth dimension. I had never heard of this frequency; I just knew that was what it was called at that time from my teaching. I had to learn the language of this frequency in yet another way. It is a language of pulses and energy, of related emotion, of feeling the different levels of communication, and of understanding the differences in frequencies.

We are taught to accept lesser truths. There are so many levels (remember the six dimensions I spoke of earlier) that all have a certain "truth" to uphold one's honour and moral stance, as we like to think of it. It is only when these levels are put together as an overview or blueprint, one on top of the other, that we can see where misconceptions, mistruths, and downright lies are.

You will intuitively receive information that has a real value to your path and purpose for being. It has to make sense to you; that is the most important factor here. If it makes sense to you on some level, then you can start building your bridge to your soul and start the flow of using instinct as your guide. You will not be wondering but rather will be knowing that something—a certain course of action—is right, even if it doesn't make sense in the first instance. This is trust when intention that is pure of thought and deed is the ultimate guideline.

I'll start at the beginning by putting my story into the pot. I will give you a short version of how I got to this place.

Yes, ladies. We have all done it, because we have the capability t see more levels of 'out-comes' and think of the long-term rather than the present only. We have allowed man to think for us, and generally organize our well-being for us, in a way that isn't natural for us to do. We have swapped our natural abilities to "know" things for man's version of seeing for us and knowing better. And we have believed them because we are coming from the heart. We are trusting and compassionate creatures who believe no one would do us harm. It's the harm itself that is difficult to see.

It has replaced the birthright we are given as the ones who communicate at the highest level for guidance with a lesser understanding which does not look at the bigger picture. Really ladies, we were naive, but the fact remains it is our fault, albeit by default, so it will be us that puts it right. And we have been given the power to do this in a way that will achieve harmony, as deep-down, ego for us does not mean being out there, proving a point. Ego to us means getting satisfaction knowing that all is well. Man mainly knows how to destroy to get what he wants and where he wants to be. If negotiations fail on a level he is prepared to go to, force is inevitable. I talk generally of those that feel the need to prove their worth in this way. That is the nature of man. Time is his enemy. We are in for the long haul, as our born nature dictates. Time is a natural element which needs respect.

I must point out that I am not a woman that hates men, and it certainly isn't the fault of any man or woman that this perception is around and being brought to the fore here as a negative in this day and age. It is aeons of misconceptions and a lesser truth that has brought about this demise, as I try to remind you from time to time.

But it has to be noted that we have had to fight for equality in ways that go against our natural instincts on how to be interpreted as the women we are. The most prominent example of how this affects women in such a severe way today mothers being forced to go to work, for various reasons. It makes us go into our minds far too often, as we have to "harden" to a world that does not seem to hold good fortune for the mother who is there to care and nurture.

Whether having to cut off from your instinct to be there for the children as the first priority is a conscious acknowledgement (it was with me) or is done so subtly that you don't realize what is happening, it does happen. Finding a true balance gets more difficult, as you have to go deeper to remove yourself from soft and loving ways that would not do you any good in the world of commerce. Suddenly, the "mother" gradually becomes the "woman" as her priorities are forced to change.

It gets more difficult to remember the mother in you, and your children can grow away from you, knowing that you can't give them the attention they need. You know deep down this is happening, but you avoid facing the issue, forcing your circumstances to be the reason you are having to do this. I know I am getting into sticky ground here with a lot of you, but please remember I am here to get all of this out into the open and help you find the way of coping with this destructive issue that goes against our innermost nature.

I will help you find a balance that will work for you and your children in the best possible circumstances. I can't give you a miracle cure overnight, but you can work with your children to find an answer, with the universe watching over you to help you too. This is something you have never had—a helping, unseen hand that will work with you to achieve what you need in the most efficient route available for you. See the universe, and it sees you.

If you can allow this thought process to open your mind up, then you cannot fail. As I have said, the guidelines of knowing what is expected of you to enter this new frequency of acceptance are simple, but they will require you to take responsibility for your life the way it has been and be ready to change the way things are once the (your) instigation process takes place.

I have digressed here a bit, as it is a particular subject that is very close to my heart and once again has bigger connotations regarding original cause and effect.

I see so many children being treated without patience and without compassion. I look at the mothers, and they look tired, short-tempered, and as though they see the children as annoyances that are getting in the way of their busy lives. Society expects mothers to go back to work quite literally as soon as they have had their baby. Society just doesn't have the time to even contemplate, and to be truthful on, the opinions of mothers I have spoken to on this subject. These mothers cannot think about what they are missing out on because it is *too painful* for them to think about. So they dismiss it from their minds, pushing their pain inward. This contributes to mothers appearing hard and uncaring.

In truth, the reverse is the case. They cannot bear the pain of the truth that they have to leave their children with a minder of some sort. The children cry and reach out for their mothers in a desperate plea for them not to be left. So the children have to learn to be cut off for from the mother too, because it is too painful for them also to be parted from the only one they know they can trust—the person who bought them into this world. I am aware that I am not the only one who knows this.

But for some reason I needed to write this down, because it is a truth that gets pushed under the carpet and is a real reason that women break off from their souls in the first place. Later down the line, it becomes a forgotten cause of depression. But one faces it either consciously or subconsciously. Breaking off from the soul *willingly*, which is how it is seen by universal law, remains with us to deal with. But we can't do this without making it a "noncaring" subject—which is not our real truth.

We have set ourselves up to fail without even realizing it. Once again, as I stated at the beginning of this, we are taking the responsibility for man's inadequacy to fulfil his duty of ensuring the well-being of the mother by providing a home for her and his child. We end up by doing all of it, but it is we who pay the cost on a soul level. And we do it willingly, apparently.

No one has done anything about this obvious truth. In fact, it is applauded when we go back to work. We make the best managers and the best decision makers, apparently. Really? I wonder why? Could it be that we throw ourselves into work to further cut ourselves off from the soul pain that is there between mother and child? Is it that the nurturing that should be going to the child is going into someone's business to make him or her richer?

As we sink our heart and soul into our work to reaffirm that we are doing the right thing by earning as much money as we can and buying our children gifts to make up for our missing soul love. All the children want is to be with their mums. But they then get used to having money spent on them to replace physical love, and then they grow up believing money is proof of success and of love, and when money is passed their way, they believe those paying them care for them, because that is the teaching of their parents.

The soul is bought for the sake of money. There are many child sex workers that believe that's what life is all about. Governments are encouraging mothers to go back to work. So what exactly is the main agenda here? It certainly is not the well-being of our children and their mothers.

All of this behaviour is utter nonsense. What type of nurturing is going to happen for children in such positions? What true bonding is likely to occur? Why has this been allowed and even encouraged? Why hasn't society made sure that mothers are treated with respect and given the support they need? Once again, it is *time* that is not being given for the children to grow with a happy mother and a happy home life. It is childminders that bring up the children, and that is a job to them. My heart cries out for all those children and the mothers that have had to break off from their natural instincts to want to be with their children every waking moment, not when our commercial society decides they should.

We have been acting as though there has been a major war on, with all women having to pull together whilst the men are at war! *What am I missing here?* These children are the future of mankind. What price are they going to put on the lives of *their* children, or on the lives their mothers and fathers when they are too old to be of use? Exactly where is their moral conscience being led? It is looking increasingly like money and fear of everything runs this level of acceptance.

Once again, this is making women responsible for the well-being of men, as they have to accept they must go back to work to help support the family home. If men cannot support their offspring, they should not be having sex that could result in pregnancy occurring. A code of respect and honour is required by both genders on this subject. That wasn't me having a "dig" at anyone. It is a fact that needs to be acknowledged and owned by those it belongs to.

Universities talk of 40 percent of all their students having mental health issues, and this figure is rising. These were the babies of twenty years ago. Is that not enough proof of where the lack of nurturing and caring started going wrong? I daresay it happened before my arrival at uni. I remember when the "free love" era came about in the sixties.

Self-respect hit an all-time low when it was an accepted fact that one could jump into bed with anyone one wanted under the banner of this new age and the circulation of drugs that was rife in this new era that glorified immoral behaviour. Am I a puritan? No. Am I someone that recognized my soul worth and found that such behaviour didn't feel right to me? Yes.

So really this stems back quite a way, and this is the result of a cavalier attitude towards life then. But look at all the addictions, alcoholism, and self-harm that is going on in society today. A lot of the older generation were in their early twenties in the sixties and seventies. It has just got worse, as the children being born to mothers from that era had an attitude of "hippiness"—of not taking responsibility for one's actions and taking life as it comes. That's just the way it was in this new era, and it wasn't fought against.

Of course, this timeline was still relatively new post-war, and those people would have been children of post-war furore at having peace in the world after the fear of annihilation.

So we can look back, blaming what's going on now upon individual actions within society as a whole. But it didn't start there. It all started at the beginning of intelligent life here on earth, as I keep repeating. But I keep finding myself writing these things, because I need to show that we are continuing this life cycle of horror for the human race. And it is now getting close to something much more sinister, which needs your attention in this most serious of ways.

We have been unable to cope more recently, and here I am talking of the gradual demise over the past thirty to forty years with regard to our rational thinking abilities. We are unable to support our senses, (meaning instincts and intuition) from the heart level and hope we all magically get to pull ourselves out eventually. But a shift is coming to totally wipe out the need for the soul connection to even exist any more, and that is the scariest thing that could happen to us.

This is not scaremongering; it is a fact which is in the interest of those that truly run this world and think only of financial gain—those who support this thinking and encourage it. The saying 'The rich get richer and the poor get poorer" has never been so apt in describing the mentality that guides our sense of today's standard of living. What price are you going to put on the future of your bloodline? Do you care? Is it up to them to make the best of their world?

Have you seen the Terminator films? They aren't far off the storyline as far as human consciousness goes. They depict on film what I can only say in words. But whereas Sarah Connor was trying to save her son because he was fighting like for like, I am getting to you first on a spiritual well-being basis to say, "Hey, wake up; we can still do this."

It is time to entertain your mind on a different level of combat. is all about fighting *your own conscience* so as not to give in to your masculine qualities at the drop of a hat, as you have probably got used to doing. It is about learning a calmer, more harmonious way to deal with situations, giving yourself *time* to respond to issues and not being bullied into any other form of decision-making. *Time* is a feminine quality, as it deals with getting things right the first time; we are in for the long haul on any choices of importance that we make.

So, this new teaching (the feminine protocol) starts with an internal overview of your attitude and your response level when faced with difficult situations. You are using yourself as the experiment of success, no one else. I am not expecting you to be responsible for anyone else's life or issues. It's just a case of looking at yourself and realizing you would really like to think better, be wiser, and start living a life in which you feel proud of being you.

To get the backing of universal law so you won't fail, you need to invoke your feminine qualities to sharpen your instincts and intuition in a way that comes from the heart. Whenever you use masculine qualities, the universe believes that you are happy with that and doesn't get involved with your decision-making, as I have stated time and time again.

How does this appear to be the case? Let me explain to make this crystal clear. When you use masculine qualities, time is not eternal; it thinks only of the present. You block any thoughts of emotion out, as I previously explained when I mentioned women who have to go back to work and leave their children with others to bring up. The key word there I used was "block".

Universal law deals with the flow of emotion, which weaves and flows as a river does. It courses through your veins to ensure a healthy body, mind, and spirit, and ultimately to ensure well-being of the soul, whose job it is to ensure its host (you) is kept in optimum health on all levels of being. When you use your masculine energy for everyday life without realizing you are doing that because it is a way of life for you, the universe does not have access to your emotion.

This is what blocking is. You are putting up a brick wall to stop any sort of pain accessing your heart through emotion. As a *temporary* measure, this is okay to do, so long as you work through your trauma and understand *why* you needed to block. Once you have learnt this new way, you can release the emotion because you have grown spiritually enough that the problem that got to you no longer has a hold over you.

The reason it no longer has a hold over you is because you keep searching in wisdom for how to keep your feminine, natural loving energy, and you keep looking for a way to use compassion or a similar quality to resolve conflict. Your feminine energy uses your masculine side as a voice to be heard by the person that needs to hear you speak because an injustice has happened, as far as your understanding has informed you. You are able to speak with a clear voice because you truthfully do not wish harm to this person. You just want to impart to him or her that you are unhappy and to speak with a truth that is calm in its words, approach, and manner. You would have taken on board the teaching in the feminine protocol's words of guidance and seen sense in the universal law section of the spiritual rules of engagement.

You maintain your femininity when you speak; you just use your masculine voice to say the words so they are clear and understood. Once you have finished the discussion (not allowing it to get heated), show respect to yourself and the other person by thanking him or her for listening, and return to your feminine self and ensure that fear is not something that is still holding you.

Know that you have done all you can to bring harmony to a situation in which there was disharmony; then leave it be. Energy works subtly, and if you return to your true natural state, the other person's energy cannot follow you. It gets left with the other person for him or her to deal with it. The universe will ensure that this is what happens, but you have to ensure you do your bit by not holding on to any "venom", or bad feelings, as this stops the process from being successful.

This is a guide. This is emotional integrity at its finest. There are many avenues on this subject, and I have attempted to bring to you a common-sense way to *start* experimenting with this better way of dealing with adversity in your life.

There is one more thing I would like share with you on this subject of feminine and masculine energy within the self. If you use your masculine energy every day, all of the time, you won't be able to pull it out of the bag to help you deal with really big issues pertaining to yourself or with situations where you might need to step in for another, maybe your child or loved one, should the occasion call for it. If you show your hand constantly, you won't have any further energy to be believed, to maybe make a difference when it *really* counts.

I have experienced all of this, and I experienced the results so I could give you a true version of what happens, and can happen, when one is faced with adversity. For this to work on the level that I speak of, you *must agree* (only to your own conscience) that you want to be guided and that you want to belong to this new level of comprehension of your life. You must want to understand the difference between knowledge and wisdom, intelligence and integrity.

4

CLUES TO A NEW UNDERSTANDING

We spend years, if not our entire lifetimes, trying to correct something we don't even know how to correct. But most of us feel it as searching for a kind of freedom that we can't explain. In those quiet moments when everything seems perfect, is it? Or is there a voice somewhere in your head saying, "What if …?" And in those rare perfect moments, how many not-so-perfect moments have there been that make this moment perfect?

When that perfect moment is there, what is really happening is that there is harmony amongst the senses. Everything feels right: the timing, the atmosphere. Your mind is in harmony with itself or another as you both (or all) desire the same outcome simultaneously—whatever that is.

It is freedom in your soul that you are searching for the connection to, and in these moments, you feel your soul is being heard and acknowledged. Do you know that only 4 percent of all relationships involve true soul mates, there for each other, who would die for each other or would live for each other because ultimate trust on all levels is the ruler of the relationship? In such relationships, no conversations are barred, no subjects are taboo, and there is no difference of opinion that won't be looked at by both parties until wisdom is found. No inhibitions are present, and there is no feeling silly or less than. There are no awkward moments, no disagreements that are harmful, and no sense that the relationship itself is greater than the individuals in it. Any children that come along are put as the first priority, and agreements are reached regarding the tone with which the children will be brought up, based on behaviour and general well-being issues.

These are true soul mates, part of the coveted 4 percent of the world. Yes, only 4 percent.

The rest of us are with someone to learn something about ourselves, and how far we are willing to go to uphold our version of love. What usually happens is that we uphold the other person's version of love while compensating, giving away our version to keep the harmony intact. Eventually we lose who we are, becoming distorted versions of ourselves that are no good to anybody. Some feel jealousy towards any offspring, leaving the children with confidence issues, as they feel the responsibility too strongly when relationship troubles are present.

We become desperate and so unhappy when we realize we are living a lie. At this point, we search for guidance in spiritual matters, thinking that others must know the answers of life and that the unhappiness we cannot explain in depth needs to be looked at to solve any problems of importance.

So you give away your energy (i.e., your trust) to those you are told to trust in. You might feel okay for a while, but all you have really done is sidestepped your soul for the moment in a bid to get yourself back to enjoy being you again. It was only part of an answer—but you never realized it at the time. How could you? No one has given you further answers on how to find the truth of your life.

It's always got to be your fault, his fault, or their fault, and so it goes on, year in and year out. You adapt, change, and reinvent yourself, believing that you have finally got to a place of happiness. You tell yourself that you must be happy. All you have done is find an alternative answer in someone else's book that says this is happiness.

Having said this, sometimes all you needed was some sort of light bulb moment that showed you the way. This usually means your soul has been able to reach you naturally or created a situation in your life that showed you something you needed to feel—an understanding that had escaped you until that moment.

If this has happened to you, you are already aware of the connection to the soul plane, the fifth dimension. You just weren't consciously aware of where that information came from.

On that note, it is sad that we are now having to re-educate our senses so we can properly assess when we are being guided towards true instinct for the right intention and not being used for someone else's purpose.

For whatever reason, you are reading this book now. You have been drawn to it, been given it to read by a friend, or heard others talk about it, and it has led to you being here with me now. You are here at this moment because you are an intelligent woman but want to know if there is more that you should know so your intelligence can be turned into intellect, the use of thought and feelings for the highest and best outcome as directed by guidance from your soul. Explained another way, you are here to become able to use your emotional intelligence so it keeps you safe as the code of the soul allows wisdom of the senses to rule all decisions that you make.

When you are truly connected to your soul, there are no lingering grey areas of thought; there are only possibilities of exploring an area which you wouldn't necessarily have explored. There are no mistakes made, only further learning and new wisdoms found. When you are in your soul, fear does not rule you; you find it interesting and perceive of it as another challenge to overcome.

All experiences, even traumatic ones, will at some point be to your advantage during your life, even if that means being able to guide another through a life drama similar to an experience you had. Similarly, it could be that observing something of a similar nature that someone else is going through opens your mind to seeing the reason or purpose that you went through what you did.

All experiences have purpose in the fifth dimension of reasoning. There is nothing left to chance; only your ability to see further as you learn to communicate through this alternative viewpoint can determine the wisdom of what has been or is happening. Total trust in the universe through your own connection will be responded to in the same way.

It is now time for me to share the me that was just like you.

5

THE CHILD GROWS UP

What I am going to do now is share my story with you, warts and all. I have done a lot of teaching with you so far, but I am a woman, a mother, and a grandmother with experiences in life that I would rather not have had to go through by choice. But I had no way of knowing just how much those experiences were going to shape my life then, any more than you do with your own story of your life now. But it will make sense to you once you start your own, new journey.

I hope this will serve as a guide for you to know what to write in your own memoirs—a must for anyone on a new path—to leave for your children that they may understand who you are and the decisions you had to make. And this you will do so they have something to read and reflect upon when they are in situations and would like some guidance on how to approach those situations they are having trouble with.

You can get your book out and just say, "Read this." You don't have to discuss it unless you want to, but reading the book will be real-time learning from someone that they know, love, and trust. It will also show that you thought of them in the past, hoping to help them on their life adventure in the future. I hope this helps you to realize that everything that happens to you in this lifetime happens for a reason. You are all needed in this war of keeping our spiritual right to be heard intact and taken seriously.

I thought it was only right to do this to show you that all experiences are part of the makeup of who we are. They determine our core learnings. We all have a story to tell, and I honestly hadn't thought about my childhood in such detail until now. Upon reflection, it was just the upbringing I needed to be able to understand the actions of those that treated me as not belonging to their community for the silliest of reasons, and the way they, in turn, were brought up.

So here we go.

I was born in 1954, this being nine years after the end of the Second World War. My childhood, I believe, was quite normal, although looking back now, I recall that I did always say I was born at the age of three, and that seemed a normal thought for me. I also remember that, when I was about four or five, the same incident happened to me three Fridays in a row. I was in the bathroom for my (then) weekly bath, and as I took my vest off, a spider suddenly appeared and ran down my arm. The exact same event occurred in the same sequence for three weeks running. It was most odd. I don't even know why I have included this; it just kept wanting to be mentioned!

School was something that I endured. I was always told by mum to keep my head down, do my work, and, if there was something I disagreed with, say to the teacher first, "I don't mean to be rude, but ..." and then say what I needed to say. I kept to this regime. Infant and junior school saw me keeping my head down. I was always petrified of tests; my mind went blank most of the time. It wasn't that I didn't know the answers; it was just the importance of the occasion, the seriousness of it all, that used to scare the pants off me.

I got okay grades. I was borderline for grammar school education. I was told that I would be expected to take another test before I would be accepted into the local grammar school. I said to Mum, "If they don't want me as I am, I am not going to prove myself to them." That was the logic of my thinking at eleven years old. I went to an all-girl secondary school, where I was bullied by a certain set of girls. I didn't live locally, and anyone that didn't automatically fit in was shunned from the pack.

I used to hide until everyone had left school in the afternoon, and then I would leave—for fear of abuse and torment, with cruel words and being pushed around. I never told my parents of this; I just got on with it. I always kept myself to myself, and the years there just happened. During the last year of school, when I was fourteen years of age, I heard that twin girls from the neighbourhood I lived in were spreading rumours that I was saying something dishonourable about a local girl having had sex with a local boy in the woods. I didn't even hang out with these people, but something in this accusation pushed a button in my mind.

I got home from school and changed into my trainers and jeans. I remember Mum asking me where I was going. I simply said, "I am going to have a fight."

She really didn't know how to respond to this, and she just replied, "Oh."

I set off without any thoughts other than that I was going to make these girls face me and what they had said.

Their mother answered the door, and I asked to speak to them. She asked me why, and I told her. She wouldn't let me speak to them (I think in hindsight she could tell my mood wasn't one to be messed with at that moment), but she said I was to leave it with her. An hour later, the mother and the twins turned up at our house, and she made them apologize to me.

The reason I included this episode for you to know about was because it was the *injustice* of the scenario that pushed my button and made me come out of a passive, well- mannered upbringing. As I put it frequently, "I wouldn't say boo to a goose." That changed in an instant because I knew I was coming from a place of pure truth. As I write this, another episode that I still remember as an unresolved injustice springs to mind.

I haven't written this previously, but for some reason, wherever we lived, Mum never sent me to the local school. This caused problems regarding friends; because I never attended the local school, I was classed as an outsider and never had friends. The children at the schools I went to had the same issues with me. Because I didn't live in the local neighbourhoods where they all lived, I wasn't spoken to much at school; the others saw me as an outsider.

This happened to all three schools I attended from the age of seven years old until I left school at fifteen. I was told by my careers teacher not to bother applying for a job in anything other than a retail shop of no particular distinction, as I wasn't good enough to get into the employ of one of the better, more prestigious companies. Looking back now, I see that this provided the perfect circumstances for my path.

When I was around ten years old, I was on my way to school when a local bully boy blocked my path. I tried to walk around him, but he continued to block me. He finally just punched me in the stomach. As he punched me, two pence fell onto the pavement. I immediately picked it up, believing it to be my two pence bus fare that Mum had given me.

The boy told me to give it to him, saying it was his. I told him no, as I thought it was my bus fare, and I held it in my hand and ran away as quickly as I could, holding my stomach, to continue my long journey to school. I paid my bus fare and got to school. It was only on the way home from school that I realized that there was two pence still in my pocket. The two pence *was* his.

I told Mum, and we took the money round to his house and told them what had happened. But it made no difference to the bully child and his family; I was branded as a thief. The children of the family used to shout out at me and follow me, and my time as a child was horrid due to the continual persecution for something I did not bring on; I had acted out of innocence and fear at the time of the assault.

They were not a nice family and were feared by most people. It was never acknowledged that the boy punched me and taunted me for no reason at any and every opportunity, and that it was this that caused the affray in the first place that led up to the misunderstanding of the ownership of the two pence.

I had no choice but to walk past this family's house on a twice-daily basis, because there was no other way to get off the estate where

I lived. These years of my childhood were truly miserable for me. These events occurred around 1963 and continued until 1966.

At home, my mum was depressed most of the time, and this air of unhappiness (I saw it as a bad mood) spilled over onto my sister and me. Although it was directed at my father, it was difficult to determine what the problem was—not that I was looking for an explanation, because it was what it was. It made me feel resented for being there, but as a child one just accepts the way things are without question.

I was cautious of her moods. Don't misunderstand me; Mum wasn't violent or abusive. She was just so pent up all of the time. She used to store up any apparent wrongdoing, as she saw it, towards her. So a lot of the time I felt as if I were walking on eggshells. As I said, I didn't question it; it was just normal and accepted as such. We didn't have a lot of money coming into the house, but Dad did what he could to always put food on the table. He was a happy-go-lucky character, and I had a very good relationship with him, and I felt Mum resented this in some way.

I left school at the age of fifteen with no academic qualifications.

There is much more that I could share here, as anyone could when remembering his or her childhood, but this just gives you a brief understanding of my beginning in life.

At the age of seventeen I was at the doctor, being put on antidepressants, clearly being seen as following in my mother's footsteps. I lived in an era when doctors dished these drugs out like sweets for any sort of unhappiness that was difficult to deal with. I really only went for some advice, and that was the doctor's solution. He said I was depressed and needed to take them. I trusted what he said because he was my doctor and I therefore felt he knew what was best for me.

By the time I was eighteen, I had a really good job. After a couple of months at my original job in a retail shop, I saw an advert in the window of the shop I really wanted to work in. The pay was nearly double what I had been getting, and I started working there the following week. Within two years, I applied for a position within the finance department and was accepted.

The manager of the office was known to be a bit of a tyrant. I used to cry in a shop doorway most nights whilst waiting for the bus to go home because I was sure she didn't like me, but I wouldn't give in. I found out later I had been put in the office to try to break down the atmosphere that one couldn't help but feel in there because of her attitude and overpowering mood. It was spilling over onto the shop floor, and no one wanted to set foot inside the office.

It was a very trying time for me. As it turned out, she did like me, and she put me forward for promotion into management within a year. Now that I can understand life from a position of clarity, I think she was just very unhappy as a person. Her home life, I found out was quite strained, but she would never admit that. I just read between the lines. I am forever grateful for the life skills she taught me without even knowing it. This just enforced my determination to succeed. I look upon her as my mentor now. At the time, though, it was awful.

I remember having an epiphany one day whilst on the bus coming home from work. This was about a year in on taking the tablets that the doctor had said I needed to take. I suddenly thought, *It doesn't matter to anyone else that I am taking these tablets because of my apparent depression, as diagnosed by the doctor. It's only me that knows it.* I realized that I was taking them as a kind of "blame" approach for my life. It seemed as if it were someone's fault that I had to take them and I was punishing that person for it. This revelation was massive.

Suddenly it became clear in my mind that I had to change the way things were. I stopped taking the tablets that day and have never taken them since. I was engaged and desperately wanted to get married so I wouldn't have to be at home any more in the depressive atmosphere there. It was time for me to move on so I could start a new chapter in my life with the man I loved.

I spoke to my fiancé that night and said it was time to arrange the wedding, and he agreed. It was January 1973, and we booked the wedding for June of the same year. I got married three weeks after my nineteenth birthday.

I had got engaged at sixteen, and life was sweet when I was with him. He was older than me by six years, and he treated me like a queen during the entire time of our courtship. He always brought me a present every Friday when he got paid. He always treated me with respect. As it turned out, I had got married to a man that had physical problems with having intercourse. In fairness, I don't believe he knew the extent of his problem either, but I did not know this until our wedding night.

You see, I was brought up in an era when one saved oneself for one's husband until the magical wedding night. That doesn't mean we didn't take part in all the other delights of sexual play; we just saved the actual act of intercourse until the right time—the night we were blessed as one. That all sounds like amazing sentiment, and it is all genuine. But that's when it became apparent there was a problem.

For a reason unknown to me then (I was just confused by the fact that he couldn't penetrate me), there was no way this was going to happen. I was so naive to the delights of this. We were both devastated, but I put it to one side and did not list it as a priority. I knew he loved me, and that was the main thing. I let my work take precedence over any personal problems. My career in office management was going well, and I was good at what I did. No one ever suspected I had problems elsewhere in my life.

After a while, we were able to get an appointment with a specialist that my husband had arranged at a top hospital, who came to the conclusion that it was my fault. The specialist said I couldn't relax enough, and he sent me to see a psychiatrist. I didn't understand this, and it wasn't what I felt was the truth, but I had no choice but to trust I was doing something wrong, because I had been told this by an expert in such matters.

The specialist sent me to see psychiatrists to find out what my problem was. Nothing changed in the bedroom; the problem was still there. Eventually the specialist we were under retired, and the new specialist wanted to try another technique to further establish what the problem was. At this point, we were coming up on three years into our marriage. His idea was to directly inject my husband with testosterone so he could identify the problem based on the response to the hormone.

From this experiment, it was clearly seen that my husband's penis expanded widthways rather than longways—proof that penetration could never have been achieved. It was decided that surgery was required to correct this. We had been explaining this for three years, but the old consultant we had been sent to had never bothered to really listen to what I was saying. It was easier for the consultant to just put it all on me.

An operation was performed, and I prayed every night (as I had done for many years) that an answer to all of this would be found. The saddest part of all of this was that, in my husbands' head, it had all "gone wrong" with me by then, and he did not even attempt intercourse—out of fear of failure, I assumed—as we had long since not discussed details.

I cannot tell you how long I cried myself to sleep with silent sobbing every night—I would say a couple of years would not be too much of an exaggeration—before I just accepted that this was the way life was to be for me.

My life adapted to me being with a man that I loved very much, but the level of intimacy that everyone else took for granted wasn't mine to have. That was how I saw the situation. I spoke to no one about this. It was, after all, the most bizarre of circumstances.

After four years of marriage, I said I wanted to have children. I had heard of artificial insemination, and I wanted to proceed along those lines. My husband agreed, and after about three years and several visits with various doctors, we went ahead with it. The doctor who performed the insemination abused me subtly, telling me that this would help my body accept the insemination as he touched me and put my hand on his crotch. This was a Harley Street doctor.

I burst out crying in the street when my husband and I got outside. I told him what had happened, as I didn't know if that was an okay thing that needed to happen as the doctor had said; it didn't feel right, and I felt deeply troubled at what had just happened. Although I was very upset, my husband said that there would be no point in saying anything to anyone, because I wouldn't be believed.

About a year later, that doctor made front-page news, as other women had come forward and complained of his behaviour. My only thoughts were ones of relief, but I should have come forward too. I didn't have the courage. That makes what I am doing now all the more important! We went to another doctor who was recommended by the hospital. She was amazing, and I became pregnant on the sixth attempt.

I eventually had two amazing daughters who were my life. I was now thirty-two years of age and was, by all accounts, a virgin mother. No one else in the world knew that. I told no one of my personal circumstances—not even my family. I felt as though it was my fault in some way, and I felt ashamed and thought I would be ridiculed if I did say anything.

I remained extremely unhappy and unfulfilled as a woman but fulfilled as a mother. I found an acceptance within me as I heard other women talk about their husband's antics of violence, verbal abuse, and generally unhappy lives. I came to an understanding that although we didn't have a sex life, my husband would never abuse me in any way.

We were harmonious in every way, shared the same sense of humour, and generally got on in many ways. I understood that most women didn't have the closeness with their husbands that we shared, but that was my price to pay. And that I genuinely believed, and I made it override any thoughts of unhappiness.

Then my world shattered. He admitted he was having an affair. The strange thing was, after the initial shock of it, I understood. I had always believed it was my fault in some way—that I was too "pure", and didn't know enough about sex or being sexy. Anyway, it had gone wrong in his head for me, but I thought that for a man not to be fulfilled in this way must be terrible.

So we parted ways, but I didn't go through the torment of the situation like one would expect. looking back as I write, I believe it was because I genuinely put his happiness before my own that I was rewarded by a sort of peace of mind that held no blame, just an acceptance. This also meant that, in a way, he had released me to be fulfilled as a woman in a future relationship with someone else.

I met my next husband almost immediately. It was a bizarre meeting. The night before my husband left me, we were invited to an engagement party at a divorced and separated club by someone that had found the right person within the group. The person I ended up marrying was the guy that ran the club.

One could use the term "on the rebound" I suppose. He had been introduced by someone I had known for many years as a good sort who was divorced and therefore also ready for a new relationship. In my mind, I heard a voice telling me that he was "the next stage in my life". I had no idea where that was coming from, and I just ran with the moment and this deep feeling that this was all an experiment.

As sex was a totally new concept for me, I allowed him to lead the way, anxious to do the right thing. My previous husband had left me with a deep emotional insecurity around sex. I told my new husband my story, which I see in hindsight was the thing that destroyed me. I let him rule me with his version of who I was as a person. He told me that I didn't know what being a wife in bed was, and if I didn't do what he wanted of me, then he would find someone else.

I had a daughter with him by this time, and I now had three children. I felt trapped. His demands on me became more perverted and included me having sex with men of his choosing. I eventually ended up not liking the person I had become. I wasn't used to drinking, and to this day, I relate drinking too much alcohol to the road to horrifying abuse. (I would imagine there are many women who can relate to this.)

He had always made it clear that If I tried to leave him, he would beat me up, and that if I tried to take his daughter from him, he would kill me. With these circumstances, I just had to bide my time and wait for an opportunity to arise (which I felt would happen) that would get me and my children away from this man.

An opportunity presented itself one day for me to escape, and I took it. I had to protect my children, as I felt there were tendencies there which were not wholesome. It was in instinct, an intuition, but I had to get out of the clutches of this man, as well as ensure my children's safety. My instincts had not been wrong, as it turned out, and my then eight-year-old daughter told me of the films that he would put on when she went to stay with Daddy, which they would watch together as she sat on his lap. They were pornographic films, from her description. The appropriate authorities were informed, and he officially was not allowed access to her until she chose to see him in my presence only. This wasn't until she was older, and only by her request.

The next twelve years were a time of learning—of finding out who I was. I had to totally come to terms with the things I had been doing, but as an adult, I am supposed to be able to say that I did those things because I chose to do so. In reality, as any woman that has been through circumstances not of her choosing knows, when you have sold your soul for love, you totally trust that what you are being told is the truth of you. I would also like to add that my children remember those twelve years as being the happiest years for them.

We all did things as a team, with decisions made in harmony. There was no man around to compete with the love and connection a mother has with her children. I felt no need to take upon myself the emotional control of a man by way of guilt-tripping them because of their own insecurities regarding proving my love.

The next period of time saw me searching for another version of who I wanted to be, having been fully aware that my life had been more than unusual up until now. I had come from being on a path of purity of spirit for the first thirty-two years of my life, and I had then been taken down a path of the exact opposite as a sex slave, where I was plied with drink to conform to the will and desires of a man who, to the outside world, was a well-educated middle-class man who attended church every Sunday.

Society saw him as a model husband and father. When I took my opportunity to part from him, he involved the local vicar to try to convince me that I wasn't thinking straight and should take him back. That phone call did not end well for him.

Once my initial strength and courage settled down from the adrenalin that all warriors must summon before they engage in battle, I had to meet myself head on. I was now thirty-seven years of age and had never ever felt so destroyed. The only worth I felt I had was that of being an object of power over other men at my husband's bidding.

Swiftly moving on from that memory, I spent the first couple of years of being unattached, still believing that sex was equal (I could take whatever I wanted and had the power to do so with my teaching from him- only he wasn't in control of it any more), and indeed I had many encounters without any form of love- just as I been taught by him to be able to cope with what I had to do to keep his love for me. The effect was that I no longer had any boundaries on self- worth that should have been there, as a woman.

I had been groomed for men by a man, but all the time now I believed that it was I who was in control. How wrong was I? What I had become was every man's perfect fantasy scenario of quick sex for the fun of it. And I was the one that had instigated it, so there was no recourse for them to have any guilt attached.

I thought that was the right way to be. I felt that I was in control instead of being controlled. But what I didn't understand was that my level of self-worth had been corrupted by all the experiences that had happened in my life. On one level—the level the world saw of me—I was strong and in control of my life, and I pitied anyone who tried to cross me.

On the other hand, I felt a loneliness that I could not describe, as though something about this was wrong, but my mind told me everything was as it should be. I couldn't explain why this unhappiness and vulnerability that I felt wouldn't go away from those deepest parts of my mind. I had no guidance, had no one to talk to, and the one friend I did talk to at the time whilst in that abusive relationship told me I must have been enjoying it, as otherwise I wouldn't have taken part. I remember feeling so knocked back by this comment, thinking, "No, she just doesn't understand."

That day made me realize that the world must see me like that, when the reverse was true. I hated it; I hated me. I also realized that no one knows what it is like to be controlled unless he or she has been there, having experienced it for himself or herself. I wanted to share all of this with you because I do understand everything you might be going through or have been through, and you don't realize that there is another level that you have yet to know about that will see you right.

6

CONSCIOUS KNOWLEDGE

Make no mistake; you will have the opportunity to take back your purity—your own God-given right to protection, your entry to your true self-worth that has evaded you all these years. Why and how? Because I have consciously made it my purpose for you to do so. You are part of my journey, just as I am part of yours. There is no attachment and no need for explanations. I know you because, in some way, you are me. But I have found all the information you need and have brought it back for you to know now.

I have been told that what I know is in advance by thirty years. This means that what I can share with you now will enable you to know now what it would have otherwise taken you thirty years to learn by the current standards of spiritual growth. You see, your memory had all of this knowledge right at its inception. But you have been taught not to access it. I will show you how to access your own spiritual DNA memory bank. This will mean an attitude of reversal of some current thinking, and some lane changing as you continue your journey.

Access to the spiritual DNA memory bank has been the biggest secret kept from us. Apart from the personal aspect of this, there is a more pressing one. We need to listen and adjust to our *original* core mentality, as the future generations *need* you to act on this now for them to have a chance of being free from control that doesn't know how to use their experiences wisely. This starts with you, but it is for the benefit of your children and the future generations of your family line too.

There has not been a call such as this since the two world wars, which saw a call on a different level. That was man calling men to arms. That was a physical war; this one involves a change of attitude that will allow harmony in every corner of the earth, with the feminine protocol attributes being the leader of ways. Now it is our turn to try to reverse the harm done by those catastrophic events.

On that note, I would like just to sidestep just for a moment and tell you of another experience I had whilst in Thailand that might add some clarity to the raw feminine emotion of the effect of war. I went to visit the war museum there, and close to the museum are gravestones for as far as the eye can see. I walked among them and found myself looking at the ages of the soldiers who lay there.

As I was doing this, my mind went to the soul plane, and what happened next was so disturbing for me that I collapsed, falling to the floor and weeping uncontrollably in front of all the other tourists. I could hear all the young men wanting to know why they were there, because it didn't make sense to them on a soul level, which was where they now were. They were all yearning for their mothers. I could also simultaneously feel all of their mothers' distress and pain at not being able to be there for their children and to protect them, which it is every mother's born right to do.

I could feel their anguish, their confusion, and their total devastation, as they couldn't be heard from beyond the grave, let alone understand why they were there. The soul plane knows only of harmony. Death in this way is abhorrent and is beyond comprehension. The ages I saw on the gravestones ranged from seventeen years to twenty-three years. The deceased were from all over the world.

Never have I experienced such emotion on such a scale. Each of those poor lads did not know how to pass the responsibility of his decision to fight back to the original cause. A lot of them died because they did not want to take another life. They decided to be killed rather than to kill. They underwent training on how to kill but not on how to deal with killing on a personal level so their souls would understand. They would have had to break off from their souls to be able to deal with the impersonal expectation that war demands of its soldiers.

The soul knows only of its owner's conduct, not the reason a decision was made. It would expect that the will of its host was given freely. It's only when you try to return to your natural-born state of purity, harmony, and compassion that it hits home, and the bridge is so vast that the spirit finds it difficult to bond with the soul because who you have become is not who you really are or where you have come from.

It was that rift, that vast space that could not be bridged, where I was feeling their pain. That link between heart, mind, and spirit was something they couldn't find easily, because they had been told only how to fight, not how to be at peace with that decision in a way that made sense to the soul. The integrity of the soul is to keep harmony among the senses.

These lads had that luxury removed, and it was replaced with a power that forced them to act against that harmony. Before they took part in physical confrontation with another, they had a war to deal with within their own psyches. This is still the case today. I have counselled soldiers that have gone a step too far, having been caught up in the moment of war.

Now, back in peacetime, their souls were interacting with them and finding those moments difficult to deal with. Their souls were asking, "Why was that necessary?" The consciences of soldiers know that somewhere something happened that did not fit into the remit they gave their souls to deal with. They can't identify where the problem is, and it results in depression or worse. There is a more detailed story of one of the soldiers that I counselled elsewhere in this book.

Once you have crossed the line on what the soul knows of (only harmony) without the proper instruction, you get stuck with the decision that you did this of your own free will. Such is the case today. Furthermore, such is the case from the smallest incident in which you harm another to the largest, as already explained. It's the same story; we have not had the continued understanding of our connections to our souls maintained in a language that keeps it pure in intention and purpose. We are using the language of trust without realizing the consequences.

Every woman will be responsible for ensuring that happiness and peace of mind are the forerunning emotions of the legacy we leave to our children and future generations. You will leave your own legacy of how you changed the world through your determination to succeed in a world full of controls on fear, and you will use your own will to enhance the desires of others. Can you see now how far-reaching this is? Can you see how immense the task is and where it *has* to go?

Yep. It is heavy; I know. I signed up for doing this for you all so you will have someone to talk to if things get rough—someone that *believes* in you without question or judgement. I am your link to your soul until you find your own wavelength to feel the guidance. I think about it as if you are attending university and I am your mentor that will be there for you. When I use the word "me", I mean my teachings, and you will have the guidance of others that have already walked the path and are ready to help you.

This new lineage of ancestry starts right here and right now, with you having been the one that was to do the right thing. Your ancestors are crying out for you to listen and become part of the biggest shift in human consciousness, as well as finding the peace in your heart that you deserve when you finally align with the next phase of growth for mankind. You may have heard of it described as the fifth dimension of humanity.

This level of consciousness allows the wisdoms of our ancestors to filter through to help us to hold our heads up in awareness. This entails not only your own ancestry but also the ancestries of those women that have been sacrificed, have died, and have taken the wrath of man so they did not and do not have to face their own shortcomings. Women have always taken on emotional torment for men. Does this sound familiar?

If you choose to learn this new way (which isn't new; it just wasn't wanted by man for us to have this connection, so the doorway was closed), then you will regain your connection to your soul through the feminine protocols that have always been there, but few have gained access, because we didn't know it existed.

The stupid thing is that we can live with man equally, harmoniously, with us both knowing our roles in society and our wisdoms reigning supreme. Instead of this, we have been taught how to downgrade our wisdom into knowledge, with man using our gift of foresight and then abusing it because he doesn't know any better. Man was not meant to know any better. That's the art of universal trust and law.

I will explain as we go along. Just keep reading for the moment.

So is there anything else you need to know about me? For instance, *why me?* Well, my initial answer is "Why *not* me?" I am just like you. But I do feel as though my life has been so diverse that it had to be so for a reason. I have always thought that. I didn't know what I meant by that, but I always thought it. During my journey since 1994, I have come to realize that, for some reason, it is my destiny to find, research, and reveal what has been kept from us.

I have constantly questioned information I have found, and each road has led back to what I have been given to understand as a truth kept from us. I just didn't realize that it would be so difficult for people to accept where my answers to their questions came from. So I stopped revealing my source; that worked much better!

In my experience, I have found that people cannot trust enough in what is being told to them. This is perfectly understandable after years of things not going right or not ending well for us. That missing equation from mind to heart just doesn't feel right either, as lies are so much easier to take and absorb than the truth.

So after many years of assessment, I now have the formula—an attitude that will allow you to gain entry to the higher frequencies, where *the* truth can be measured against the truth of your life up until now.

I can gain access to your path and explain the *true* message that your soul has been trying to tell you, to get through to you, in its many disguises of dramas that occur in your life and the chance meetings, songs, films, overheard conversations, illness, and diseases (the list is endless) that might give you a clue that a change of attitude is needed for you to progress towards happiness.

This new pathway will cut out most of that having to happen, as you will be able to tune in to your own soul and *feel* the right way for you.

You will be able to adapt, hear, and use the intuition that accompanies this level of acceptance.

All you will need to do is trust yourself—and that is the first lesson on how to do that! To be quite honest, if you have had the wrong guidelines on what life is all about, how can you trust your present instincts on what is right? *Huh?* I know because I have been there, and I refused to listen to start with. Hence my scientific nature has been weaving constantly throughout my experiences to ensure that what I *thought* I was being told was true.

It was a continual flow of being pitted against what I was *feeling* was true. I have had to check out all possible pitfalls to be able to know how to guide you through them. Thoughts and feelings are worlds apart. I will write in more depth on that later.

This first part of this book was intended to let you see *me* (and I so hate talking about myself) and how I got to this state of needing to give you the opportunity to understand that all women are my purpose, and that I started this from very humble beginnings. I have faced all sorts of adversity to stop me from bringing to you this biggest secret from the rule book on universal law and what that means for us as the female gender.

I have done everything humanly possible so I can be there for you, walk with you, and show you that you are not alone with this massive quest that the universe has asked you to be part of with me. It would appear we are being given an opportunity to put this unequal state of soul worth right. That's what I have been fighting for. I know that I have been given the green light to bring this to you now. After years of soul slavery, you are to be given the reprieve that excites your soul the most—an opportunity to be heard.

You didn't cause this, but unless we, as women, make a

commitment to ourselves and our future generations that we *insist* on being part of the cure of the degenerative universal consciousness that has taken hold of our senses globally, it will be too late for future generations to pull themselves out. This present consciousness puts who you are seen to be in society above what you are in the soul aspect of humanity's greater view of your worth.

There is little hope for humankind to be anything but batteries for the chosen few who have elevated themselves and have made others believe they have the right to their positions of hierarchy. This has a great parallel to the Matrix trilogy, if you are interested in learning from that perspective. All films of this nature have been produced to prompt us to read between the lines and to confirm within our own thoughts that we are not alone in feeling something just isn't right.

In 2004, I thought I was ready to start a business to help those who had suffered emotional traumas in their lives that they needed help with. I had, after all, been studying my subject for nine years, and I had secured my connection. I had an office in a prime location and advertised in magazines and generally put myself out there to be seen. What I didn't know was that there was a loophole I hadn't thought about. Once again, naivety and trust brought me crashing to the floor. I lost my office, my home—everything that one would usually feel secure about.

My ego also believed this must be the way I was to get myself known. I hadn't thought big enough. It wasn't until this happened that some of the most profound understandings started to flow. Everything that happens is meant to until sufficient knowledge is gained in the fifth dimension.

I knew I had done something wrong for this to happen, and I realized, to my cost, that there was an area I hadn't checked on. I had taken this level for granted. I don't need to share the details of what happened, as it really was just a drama that presented itself to stop me in my tracks. But I hadn't thoroughly checked it out on all the levels that it needed to be checked out on. I was not told of what I was doing wrong. I had to work that one out for myself. It was simple, but it took another five years for me to work it out. It was a simple protocol—a respectful acknowledgement—that did not come from me, though it was for those that I was allowing access to so they could solve their problems. Above all, I was once again giving my trust away without proper protocols in place. I knew nothing of protocols at this stage; I hadn't given them a thought. But I was running with the hierarchy of our deepest intentions and those that protect and guard the gates to this.

There are rules. I needed to learn about them and implement them into my work. But I learned this through financial suffering as well as well-being. I never lost faith in my connection with the fifth dimension; I just knew that whatever was happening to me was happening for the right reason. Such was my belief in my path. What I was being taught to know was fourfold.

I was again trusting in others that did not have the same purpose or intention set as their highest priority as the one I had. In reality, how could they? My path was a lonely one which I had to travel alone. Also, degradation and humiliation came with this (including financial ruin, the loss of my home, and having to beg to be rehoused by the local council and being refused). I had never had to suffer the consequences of failure (as society sees it) so deeply as I did then.

There were times when I had to dig really deep, but time brought a solution once I had had gone through that and other degrading actions that I instigated whilst in a different mindset. How could have I allowed this to happen? My blood pressure was extremely high at this time, and my doctor prescribed some medication to lower this. He put me on such an increased dose that it severely impeded my thinking process. I only found this out because, during on one of my check-ups, I saw another doctor who questioned the dosage of the drug I had been prescribed. I had become fearful of my situation; I was hiding in the bedroom when mail arrived, knowing it would be letters from debtors, and I was scared of the phone ringing for the same reason.) She changed the brand to one that would suit me, and that did the trick with a small dose.

Whilst in the previously mentioned "medication control", I made some very unwise decisions that I wasn't proud of. But as I previously stated, I never lost faith or belief in my purpose. That's all that needs to be said here.

So it appears I had to go through degradation, and humiliation. I lowered my self-respect boundaries, and I lived in fear. We all make mistakes, but the universe will make sure you stick to the path once you have committed to it. It is after all, ensuring that your well-being on the soul level is learning, evolving, and will always see you right if you continue to believe in yourself and what you have committed to.

As I say frequently throughout this book, believe in the law of the universe, the highest truth, and it will believe in you equally. The universal truth has no bounds on trust; it hears every decision you make and knows why you made that decision. My decisions were made because I was short-circuiting what was destined for me by the rules of man's hold (via their original blueprint) on my destiny as a woman.

The masters of universal law that were guiding me cannot interfere with my free will, but they can ensure I learn what I need to before pulling me out of the demise that other women who are not connected would probably never get out of the cycle of. Opportunities present themselves for you to take; it's then up to you if you want to take them. That's how this works. It's all very clever and very real, and those feelings of inspiration that you get from time to time will be your guide. It's all such an adventure.

If you can remember this, nothing will get to you on the real deep levels of soul worth. Keep believing in the commitment you have made for yourself, and the commitment you have made to your children to guide them to a truth that far exceeds what society sees as the story of you, and you *cannot* fail in your mission to succeed.

Wisdom always rules. Keep searching; it is always there.

Now I am taking you back to the original cause of my demise regarding my intention to start a business with my knowledge and connection, believing that was the way forward at that time, as there is more I think you should know that will help you. This is also important to remember: This entire book will have bits in it that really hit home. You are not alone in your world of dramas. They are just *your* dramas to learn something that will help you or your loved ones, but that is all. Try to remember every morning to ask for help and to thank your link through this teaching. (I will explain why that's important later.) It will strengthen your connection for yourself and prove you are still on the path which is now yours by right. So, as I said, back to the cause.

I was not asking my clients to adhere to any form of responsibility to be able solve their problem once I had given the information that they wanted. I hadn't taken seriously enough the *responsibility* of what I was doing or where I was going. I was being so naive, even after the years of training I had already gone through. It was such a delicate, simple understanding, but because I knew the rules of entry, I used to go there and retrieve the information required for the client.

My *trust* was such that they would use this information with integrity. But I didn't make my understanding clear to them that this information was to be treated with respect. They were not responsible if my insights got distorted if they chose to pass that information on in conversation in a way that was not kept in gratitude or appreciation when such valuable insights were given.

Hence, the downgrading of information that was given in wisdom could be reduced to a gossipy conversation of knowledge, causing distortion and resulting in disrespect and dishonour for the soul plane.

The disrespect that was resulting because of my naivety was something I would have to endure in my own life at the level of integrity I had called upon. I had entered a place that deals with the purest of truths, and I was not ensuring the protection and sanctity of where this information came from. I wouldn't be able to once the client had left my office. I had charged a fee for the consultation too, which made it worse. I hadn't then understood the full implication of my path.

It was right that I had to take this disrespect and dishonour, because I had instigated the cause. On this level of soul worth, I had to be made aware that I understood the implications of falling short of the intention of those that protected me from this precious realm. I did not know this at the time; I knew only that there was something I needed to go through.

What I understood was this: once you have started earning money at a certain level of awareness, your mind becomes comfortable with that and you stop looking for an increased level of awareness that is there for us all. The wisdom of the soul plane was going to ensure that wasn't going to be the case for me. I had originally asked for me to be able to reach every woman and to be able to offer an opportunity, a choice, to pull them out of misery and forgetfulness of their true worth—and this was what I was going to be kept to. The masters who were my constant spiritual companions and guides were going to ensure my success—when the time was right. They weren't going to let me fall short of my own intention via the trap of turning this into a business at that level, which they showed me by way of a simple misunderstanding. There was far more I needed to experience.

I received the wisdom I needed. Wisdom is delivered with hindsight until you are able to see it in foresight. Trust is also required, as well as tolerance, patience, and a willingness to listen to instinct and intuition. That wisdom taught me where to look for the red herrings that crop up in life. It's not that they will stop appearing; it just means that you can keep a certain level of awareness on your intention and purpose, alongside where an experience is taking you.

Accept that whatever is happening is meant to happen, until you fully understand that you don't need to go through it again. It sounds contradictory, but the subtle levels of choice are quickly understood by your instinct as you increase this feminine value in its true worth.

There is a personal responsibility attached to any spiritual soul growth. The format—the agreement to take responsibility for your life, which is acknowledged in this book—protects you as well as the overall purity of the soul plane and the frequency that is able to be kept open because of your acknowledgement of and taking part in this new wisdom.

This is all *conscious* understanding. Until now, the majority of people get thoughts in their heads about things, but they don't really know where those thoughts come from. There has not been an awareness, such as the one I am here to teach, on how to decipher those messages that your soul is trying to help you hear.

An insight can get distorted if discussed with another whose mind is not open to the instinct and intuition of the soul. I learnt this earlier at my own cost, before I had my mind opened consciously. It cost me dearly in time. I had to wait a year before the same opportunity presented itself for me to go forward because I listened to a friend's version of truth rather than stick to my instinct.

Anyway, getting back to the final bit in my story timeline of realizing that I was not meant to carry on with the business attitude that I had developed by way of clients paying for my services, I stopped physically working with clients and just continued on my own path, which was presenting quite a few changes. I decided that, for the moment, it was time for me to be given further teachings, or "experiences", that would strengthen my connection, allowing me to be there for all women to ensure no stone would be left unturned in being able to secure answers for anyone with a troubled mind that crossed my path.

Protocols (safeguards) were something I hadn't taken into account, owing to naivety on my part seventeen years ago. I knew the core of the information was true at this stage; what I hadn't understood was that it could still be open to abuse, albeit unwittingly. There was a loophole that could be used, and probably was and still is, by those that know how to bend individual laws on spirituality.

When the original concept of the soul frequency, the core of the fifth dimension, was founded, the intention was to keep us within the natural boundaries of human consciousness and the human qualities of growth, keeping the core intention of equality and harmony in place as the highest outcome for intention and purpose.

It was the ultimate guideline—the key to keeping us protected in the purest of ways from all aspects of corruption through abuse of our trust. It was a hard lesson to learn. It has taken until now, and I have been made to go over all my teachings again to ensure I don't follow the same unchartered territory, where I would have spent my life taking the toll of the mentalities of others that weren't fully understanding of the purity of the level that I was accessing to give them peace of mind.

I am having the feeling as I write this that something akin to this has happened before, adding to the demise of our soul worth. The masters of our well-being, the ultimate gatekeepers to this frequency, this level of comprehension, have also ensured that I have left no stone unturned in bringing to you this unseen truth that has been kept a secret from us for millennia.

If you look at my timeline of experiences, you will notice that there was always more that I needed to *feel* to make this real. Even from the level of my teaching, which came from the highest of teachers, I had to feel for myself the most profound understandings, by searching in places that are there to see for the looking with a certain eye for truth.

It could be a thought put into my head or a strong urge to follow an instinct; that was all I had to go on. It still is, and even as I write now, I am being shown a deeper truth to relay to you—one that wasn't there at the beginning of my writing this book. Bringing clarity to those instincts was mine to make happen. Something inside of me said to start writing. The end of the book wasn't even in sight, but I had to begin and trust in the guidance that has never let me down.

History is made by people acting on something they believe is right to do. There was never any written rule book. Even this book cannot make decisions for you. It can show you how to look for clues. I have written this book because I was determined (a strength I got from my mother, but in a different, unseen way; she works with me still from beyond the grave) to give you an opportunity to set the record straight on the story of you and how you will pass on knowledge to your children, and your children to their children and the future of your bloodline.

You will be remembered as someone that refused to just go with the flow of who people think you are. You will be remembered as someone who took an oath, made a commitment, to ensure that the teachings of mankind were made right by an army of women. Your conscious understanding of a new set of rules will stop you making "mistakes" and being on a loop of your past and the story of you.

Until now you have been naive, but the truth of your naivety will be passed back through the generations of women in your family so they can help you now to succeed where they could not help you before. Naivety, it appears, is no longer an option, as there are too many clever minds feeding off of the naivety of others that truly believed they were helping the world evolve into a better place.

I have put in place these protocols I spoke of earlier for your protection too so you will be safe as you grow and will not give your precious gift of new energy to someone who has not agreed to grow at the same level you will grow to, without having taken the vow of trust required by this teaching. We are not here to carry each other; we are only to be there for others as they grow in their own time, pace, and way.

If you do get drawn into another's pace of learning that doesn't match your own, you will know. You will feel tired and will find yourself thinking of them, worrying whether they are all right and feeling drained. This is your clue that you have put someone else before yourself, and this is your choice to make. But haven't you been doing this your entire life to date? It's time to be conscious of those you help and of why they need your help—why they need your will to support their lack of control over their own.

It could just keep them there, but now they are using your energy to help with personal gain, which is nothing the soul plane can use. You are merely giving away your free will to another, for them to achieve a personal desire of someone with no direct contact with you. Trust me; I could write a book of my own just on this very subject of giving my worth, my will, away to help others in their causes, whatever those may have been. But when it came to me asking for help, no one was interested in helping me to achieve what was important to me. All of the promises, intentions, and agreements meant nothing. There was always a *reason* they could not return the favour—even if I was desperate for help. So let me say here and now that it's time to move on and learn how to change *your* future!

If you think that sounded callous, compassion is all-encompassing and does not leave you feeling drained. It gives freedom for all parties to use the universal love frequency for growth and protection. This is something you will learn in time. Worry is born out of fear. There is no end to fear; it is an energy sapper' of the first degree. Learning about compassion and all its attributes in the right way will shift your understanding of just about everything that you care about. I will help you with this. It really is a game changer.

So my trust is in your soul to hear this message and join this movement towards camaraderie, this campaign, this determined effort to get ourselves back into being the powerhouses that we are meant to be. I say all of this, but it isn't a physical movement where you will be expected to march with placards and banners! This is subtle, making your own life work for you. No others need to know of the decision you have made to become part of this unless you tell them.

I warn you it will not always be easy. The reward will be the sense of freedom you will feel as you reach a level of understanding that will make you feel as though you are part of a oneness you have never experienced before.

There is a vast number of feminine souls waiting in spirit to help you achieve this state of well-being. Some of them who have passed from this life you might know personally. Some you may have heard of in history; they, in their own way, have been the forerunners of this movement—this shift of consciousness. We are all one movement. And it all starts with you now, for your lineage of future generations to be part of the universal message and for you to know that you did your bit. You were willing to learn.

Are you ready to learn some amazing truths—ones that will change your life forever? I say this with caution. You have to be committed. And if you can't see for yourself that you are worth it, do it for others for the moment, until the pace quickens and you reach your own level of purpose.

I also want to mention something else so you can perhaps have more clarity on what is available through this level of conscious awareness and be excited about the prospects that await you.

I have crossed paths with those with those who have suicidal tendencies, deep depression, and so much guilt after having an abortion; those who have suffered miscarriage and addiction problems; those with relationship difficulties (with themselves or others), including those in mother–son relationships, mother–daughter relationships, abusive relationships in general, and sibling relationships; soldiers returning from war; learned people; and businesspeople. I have visited abused women's safe houses and examined religious beliefs that have been controlling outcomes. The list is endless. The result is always the same: the releasing of emotions that should never have happened. This has kept you a prisoner of your own mind for far too long.

All of those whom I have helped were, for a short while, allowed entry into the frequency that showed me exactly why they were so troubled. At that point of discovery, they understood how to go forward from that point with revealed information that could be used to make sense of actions taken by others towards them or to understand their own actions towards others. As I decipher the experiences for an understanding to be seen, it changes the way things need to be remembered. It also changes the future, as my clients are able to let go of any intense horrid memories which hold on to their energy in a destructive way. By allowing this alternative viewpoint, flow, and regrowth happen. This converts into strength, confidence and self-worth as the deciphering continues each and every day, giving continued insights.

It's always a different question, but it all progresses to the same level of understanding—that of a basic truth that no one is taught the real situation as far as our senses (which are connected to our souls) are concerned. The most important thing for those I have helped was that I used their words and their explanations and showed them all a different way of looking at the situation with the increased knowledge I could give them. This works. This connection is there for you too, so you can begin to look at your life in a different way. As you become part of the connection, a whole new set of explanations opens up to you, revealing hidden knowledge.

Everyone has to abide by a certain rule before I enter the frequency of where all knowledge is known and all secret feelings are felt. They have had to agree to keep that knowledge sacred—whatever it is that is revealed in that moment of the meeting of minds. None have hesitated, because turmoil and chaos are in control of their emotional state when they come to me for guidance; they have been in a living hell for far too long.

I only ever know my clients by a name they choose to use; no records are kept. The consultation is one of a soul meeting where earthly records do not come into play. In fact, it would be dishonourable for such knowledge to be personally known and recorded outside of our meeting and discussion therein.

The fact also remains that, in truth, once they have left my company, the personal link to the frequency is disconnected from me to them, and I have no knowledge of, or desire to, keep personal contact details of anyone. It is only the experience of a soul that has been enlightened that is of any worth to me. It is of no consequence or use to anyone else who lives in the truth of the soul plane to hear details of anyone else's right to be heard.

Every single living soul behaves according to the truth of his or her life so far regarding the truth of how he or she will continue living his or her life. Their guidance comes from their own experiences. Now a new truth can be given which upgrades the experiences to be seen in a new light. They have the same memories, but they now have new knowledge about what they were meant to learn from their past experiences.

I have done my best to write this in a format that will open your mind to a powerful belonging that can only be felt. I will commit now to giving talks globally and personally answering questions that you may find difficult to resolve. I will provide information on that later. As I said, I am here for you!

Well, I think that is just about everything I can tell you in an overview of what it is possible to achieve. I have tried to diversify everything in various areas to give you some idea of the choice to learn, to grow, and to change from who you are now to who you can be with the correct guidance.

The world cannot wait any longer for things to just naturally occur. This has to be done *now* if we are going to give future generations any sort of chance of succeeding in this mammoth task. But at least we do still have a chance to change what is to become of our children's future and the lives we personally have left to live. And you will know you did your bit to ensure that your family line will have the right and best chance of survival in this world that has lost all sense of sanity.

It is your choice; it always has been. It's just that now you will know the truth about the things you allow to happen being for the right reason for the best outcome for all concerned. Everything you do from this moment on has a new set of rules on choice. It all starts here and now.

Are you ready to turn your whys into wisdom? Are you prepared to join a growing camaraderie amongst women who have already given their pledge to ensure handed-down knowledge through the generations to come has true validity and will ensure true worth and true freedom of the will of the individual?

I am truly excited for you! I love it when I get told, "Ah, that makes total sense as to why …"

As women (the feminine), we need to do this so man (the masculine) gets to know his place and regains his honour. We cannot believe ourselves to have succeeded with our men if they do not follow us as destiny commands, but we cannot insist. If they do not follow our new way of giving respect reciprocally, that is up to them.

But you will grow regardless. Your self-worth will increase, and you may well leave man behind as you recognize your new worth as a woman, a wife, and a mother who needs to be looked at as though she is amazing and worth behavioural changes. But remember: we have to start and persist in this new regime. In essence, this means respecting your body and allowing your soul to help you to understand that this is your temple. Those you give access to need to be worthy of that access. Do not underestimate your femininity. Give yourself as much time as you need to truly understand yourself through compassion and how to apply it to *yourself* first. Do not let control through sympathy get in the way. This is your soul worth you are fighting *yourself* for. Once you have felt the contact reestablished with a new code of conduct, a new you will emerge.

The decision to belong to the future of mankind or be left in the dark ages is up to one's individual mentality. We have to recognize that our own revised boundaries have to come first. If we do not allow this, we leave our boundaries open to abuse and the whole cycle starts again, and we have to go through it all one more time.

It will all be done with compassion through wisdom. Take three deep breaths: one for your mind, one for your heart, and one for your spirit. Be excited; your soul is waiting for you to hear its messages in a truth you have never understood before!

But first, a riddle which comes directly from the soul (fifth) dimension to help you on your journey. If these words make you think, you are ready to learn.

What is it that we need to see—
The way forward, or what will be will be?

Is it the answer that fools us all, or the question
that's so unrealistically tall?

We have the answer; the eye can find
(through veils undetectable) if you are kind

To all living things who are greater than we:
The sea, the birds, the great healing tree.

The fifth dimension is there for us all;
To find the clues, begin very small.

The first time you visit will send you reeling;

To see clearly with the heart is a mind-blowing
feeling!
Can you not see?
Can you not feel?
The greatest gift is the mind—so real.

Make it command your thoughts first (until it is
disciplined well),
Then let your heart take over; ahh ... it begins to
swell.

What more can I say?
Your travels may be far,
But the rewards are great ... What an adventurer
you are!

To open your mind is to open a door
To go further than you ever knew possible before!

Do you understand now?
Am I getting the message across?

Or are you to settle for being told what to think
and do,
And risk suffering a great loss?
Annette Rose, as channelled directly from the fifth
dimension, April 2001

7

GETTING YOU STARTED

To help get you started, there are a couple more things that you need to acknowledge, and this next paragraph is most important, as it allows reason to be the leading thought on everything. This is yet another level, another viewpoint—an alternative way of looking at the same subject from a different perspective. What I am constantly trying to achieve (maybe not in the most efficient of ways, but it flows, and I write) by going backwards and forwards and trying different approaches is a method of providing alternatives. Certain phrases, understandings, and revelations will suit different personalities who are at different stages in their spiritual understanding of life.

What I am going to express is an important fact to remember. It is the absolute right of your soul to expect this code of practice from all others that live on this planet. If you do not receive it from another, calmly observe that this is a failing on that person's part, not yours, and say no more. Do not talk of important matters with someone who shows no understanding of your innermost feelings, because that person is not aware of the level you are going to be making decisions from. Without this being in place to start with, nothing can, or will, change for anyone. This is where the learning starts. I will guide you through each bit.

This explanation of the return of manners, morals, respect, and honour for the soul aspect of our core being, is to be allowed to rule all of our emotions. It is this level that this teaching is about.

Collectively, there has never been a teaching quite like this on the level I am explaining to you. The riddle that was given is all about the soul's quality and ability to look deeper, more calmly, and more intuitively into areas of your life that have been giving you a totally different set of emotional causes and responses, as you were not aware of this greater level of existence before.

What you are going to read about is how to reinvent yourself by understanding your own life and the choices you have made prior to this teaching. Everything from now on can have a different outcome, as it allows more choices and more levels of acceptance to be made known to you. This next part is the most important part, as it is connected to the highest authority, which oversees actions, responses, and wisdom through understanding. It takes into account that you were unaware of such an authority being in existence that will work with you all the time you work with it. Your permission is required to take part in this, and it then becomes your responsibility to ensure you will do all you can to uphold this precious new lifeline that is yours by birthright, though you have been denied its existence until now.

Let me be clear for those that fear this will interfere with religious beliefs. There is *no way* that this teaching interferes with the *core concept* of religion. Religion is there to help us with our spiritual enlightenment. This teaching comes from the inception of life before all religions and is the cornerstone of all faiths and beliefs.

There is *not one* religion that overrules this teaching; it was instigated *before* different factions of religion came about. Therefore, it does not go against any religion. If anything, it is the forefather of religion. It is man that may have lost his way in the purity of the teaching. My purpose is to re-educate your senses so you can see for yourself the misalignment of some previous teachings and so you can understand why things may not seem true from your understanding of life.

Those that feel as though something is wrong, as though they are not understood, and that have problems with religion and its present teaching will find peace with this new way. Why? Because it is imprinted on our souls; that's why. But there are few teachers that keep the lifeline to the soul going, and mankind and its wars have seen to it that purity is something of a dirty word amongst those that truly seek the highest answers.

I am not against religion; I am only against the extended control it exerts upon each and every soul that comes into contact with a doctrine that does not feel right. In this new fifth-dimensional teaching, there are basic rules that are at the heart of any religion, and they are the only ones that are true and in alignment and harmony with the soul.

Your chosen religion comes after this teaching and is able to run in harmony with it and should serve you well if it gives our feminine aspect the respect and honour that we deserve and that is our birthright to expect. For those that are not religious, these rules are all anyone needs for guidelines on how to live life in harmony. They date back to the beginning of time itself.

The very reason this book, and my continued work, is necessary is because the lack of proper guidance on personal conduct is not globally accepted on one level. Women are suffering because men are not finding it within themselves to work together to find peace on a global frequency. The proof of this is easy to spot. How many religions, faiths, and beliefs are there? What is available has always been produced by, or come about because of the interpretations by man of God.

The whole point that has been totally missed is that religion in all forms was intended as a way for men to learn how to behave towards men, remember. Woman were never part of any necessity to be "taught" anything. We have always known that we are protected, because we have to be. God expected that code of conduct to be carried out by man towards us, knowing our high value and worth. But for that we would have to be acknowledged as such, consciously.

I further believe that an oversight from those responsible for introducing the original moral code into our minds (spiritual DNA) took it for granted that man, without question, would always understand of women as those that gained access to the gods, or creators so they would be revered as the ones that needed to be listened to because of their feminine ability of communication to the higher, unseen realms of existence—the place of high regard, respect, and honour for our instincts, intuition, and knowing, and the reasoning that we are capable of knowing.

Religion was indeed invented by man to rule itself, by itself, to ensure women kept their rightful place as the communicators of the soul plane, where all wisdoms are found, which stops us all having to repeat bad calls. Our capabilities of foresight allow harmony of the senses to be kept in balance, so informed decisions have always been available as the main priority for prosperity and well-being.

The communication breakdown—the misrepresented view of our importance and—and I hate to say this—quite probably the assumption of such magnitude that these facts were known to man and didn't need spelling out could have been the original cause of our demise. We began to lose the power of our instincts and our right to being honoured for our feminine status.

And because of this oversight, this communication breakdown, it was taken for granted that women were to use their abilities, their free will, for man at his bidding as an expected right. So what does this mean now in the long term for us? These further, more up to date analogies keep the picture of the mistakes made in the past clear for the current reason for re-education.

The most disturbing outcome of this is that women are suffering continually, and if women suffer, so do the children. So I am standing up to change things. I am calling time, in agreement with those that guide me.

You have to know that you are worth it, that your children are worth it, and that their children will be worth it. It's time for our suffering to be held to account, and that of the many generations that have gone before us. For the misery that this has meant for us needed to be consciously acknowledge by the hierarchy of universal law in its wisdom that we have been unable to connect to our true power of intention for harmony to rule equally, but differently. Man has a different quality to bring to the table than we do. We apply a logic that does not feed the ego for supremacy in its own right.

You see, Man would not know how to do this; it is difficult for him to separate from his ego in the way woman can. Woman has her strengths in the world of emotion, where reasoning is entwined with outcome. It is not part of man's spiritual DNA to be able to do this; The responsibility has fallen to us to fully understand what is required. It's not man's fault; it has always been our responsibility to take control of the long-term plan for the sake of humankind's future.

What our role is in this new way is to see where a certain course of action could or will lead to, and to ensure we have acted for the best possible outcome whenever possible, for all parties that need to be considered when making decisions. But the children must come first in priority of action regarding knowing their needs.

So that's what this is all about. Stand up and be counted as one that is willing to be assessed and to reassess personal conduct (actions and reactions) so you know you are working with the many that have gone before in a positive way. If we do not do this, humankind will cease to exist. Our free will would be too far gone to retrieve.

It will be a forgone conclusion that you are happy to continue to give your free will to another entity that has not got you or your children in mind when orders of behaviour and "the way things will be" continue to be introduced to us subtly so we don't see them coming. We just accept this, the way we always do.

I hope you are able to trust what I am telling you on this whilst you are reading. By all means, I expect you to check it out with your own research. But I also know that today's woman is kept far too busy to cheque things out in the same depth with the disciplined research that I have given this for over twenty-five years. That, too, is all part of the plan for those that wish to remain in power. This happens when you haven't got your mind on what you are giving away, which is the area that truly counts.

The benefits of this new fifth-dimensional way of thinking, which includes the guidelines of good manners, morals, honour, and respect, is the only way forward to regaining your free will so you will feel it, understand it, and make it work with you and for you. It interrupts the flow of those that have always controlled you or to whom have given your strength without realizing it. It brings a whole new concept of "I am, I will, I will not" into an internal strength as this DNA strand that is within us starts to strengthen and make itself heard for the first time.

To follow is an up-to-date version agreed to and written by me whilst in a total oneness of communication from the purity of the soul plane (the fifth dimension) to help us now, written in a language that is modern and understandable for our time frame.

This is an agreement which gives you the right to universal justice and the right to be heard. Once agreed to by you (you need only say yes to yourself—that's all) it takes into account all of your own behaviour towards yourself and others to date. From today, there is a new you!

Read and ensure you understand what is being asked of you. There is no trickery involved in this! It is a spiritual "drawing of the line" of you on every level. Everyone has to do this (yes, including me) to make it count on all levels of being. It will also help you to remember that you are not saying you are perfect, but the system is.

It is saying of you that you care enough about your own future, the future of those you love, and even the future of those you have yet to meet or never will, to do your bit in helping the human race to bring about a set of boundaries that have never truly been in place in this way to ensure that equality through harmony is the main priority.

What is being offered to you is a chance to have your life counted and to have your soul get the recognition it deserves for undertaking such an enormous task. But also understand this: it is only *your* life, *your* understandings, and *your* conduct that you need to be concerned with. It is up to others to be responsible for their behaviour towards you.

I am here to guide you towards an increased level of awareness, which has been concentrated to ensure that the right information is being given to you to succeed and to join those whom I have crossed paths with on a personal basis. This is the first time I have attempted to do this on this massive scale. I have had to do this in this way as there is no time left to do it any other way if we are going to save the children of tomorrow and teach them what their heart is truly for.

What I know for certain is that I am not wrong. The people I have brought peace of mind to with this information know I am not wrong. It stays with you for the rest of your life. Your agreement now will be your official joining. It never leaves you. You will be part of the biggest community on the planet. You will be part of the future of a humankind without compromise.

You will have access to soul wisdom to stop you having to go through the horrors of repeated bad choices (unless you choose to do so). There is no control; you need only free your mind from control over it that is interfering with your own wisdoms and knowing. This way teaches harmony without compromising your soul worth.

Step 1: Initiation

When you are ready, look at my picture on the back cover briefly, and then look at the picture on the front cover of this book and commit it to memory. Put your right hand over your forehead, shut your eyes, and say inwardly, or out loud if you prefer, "I am ready to be initiated into the feminine protocol's link through the soul reiki frequency of love, law, logic, and language so I can go forward with wisdom as my guide."

(Note: S.O.U.L reiki is a registered trademark which stands for; the Source Of Universal Love, Law, Logic, Language).

After a full minute has passed, remove your hand from your forehead, assume the same pose as the one depicted on the front cover, and hold it for at least two minutes, but take as long as you want on this as you think about your new conscious commitment to the soul plane, yourself, and the sisterhood. Feel the comfort as you recognize that you have now become part of what is potentially the biggest "belonging" on the planet.

Please note: A certificate of confirmation that you have been initiated is available with your name on it for £10 as a download.

Please also confirm that you agree to the universal justice authority and the code of conduct. If you would like a bespoke one with your name written by hand on quality paper, it will cost £25, which includes P&P to your address, wherever you live in the world. Email me in the first instance for further details at thefeminineprotocol@ gmail.com, with the heading "certificate request", along with which service you require, the details of your name as you wish it to appear, and your mailing address.

For the Man in Your Life and Any Male Friends

For all men that are in favour of the Feminine Protocols aims and intentions for every human being to re-align the senses, the initiation is slightly different. Please ask him to follow these instructions:

> Put your left hand on the picture of the hand on the inside cover at the *back* of this book and visualize the symbol on the hand in the image being transferred to your right hand, which you are to place over your forehead with your fingers pointing upwards so the palm of your hand is on your forehead. Hold this position for two minutes. Visualize that the symbol is a blessing and know that you will gradually respond over time to the energy being emitted through this symbol as it is activated, helping you regain the true role of your masculine energy.

The aim of this is to prompt you to see each other with fresh eyes in a way you have never before been able to. This will allow you to express emotion as something to discuss with each other without attributing blame, which will enhance the qualities already within your relationship and within the self.

Once the instructions above have been carried out, the man has agreed to become a *protector* of the sisterhood. This means that he can be acknowledged as such. The next two steps apply to him too. A certificate of soul reiki initiation is available through fifthfloortechniques@gmail.com with the heading "soul reiki certificate request," with the man's name and a confirmation that he has completed the initiation and agrees with the rules as set out by the universal justice authority and in the code of conduct. The same fees apply: £10 for a download, £25 for a handwritten name on quality paper sent to you anywhere in the world. For the bespoke handwritten certificate, do not forget to include an address.

You are now ready for step two, the conscious agreement between yourself and universal law.

Just turn the page and continue the initiation.

Step 2: Universal Law Authority

The Fifth Dimension (Soul Plane) Universal Justice Authority Conscious Code of Acceptance

I believe in the protection and authority of universal law (the primary code of the soul), which exceeds and expands on all other forms of justice.

My life is controlled by the freedom and restriction that this influence governs.

I will be free to experience all that I need to for my own personal growth and the growth of humankind.

No other individual has power over the decisions I make or the way I present myself.

Absolute truth is the highest outcome, as it is governed by the pure intention of the soul.

I will live my life by these rules, as it is only my soul I am answerable to.

My soul is part of the universal soul, which ensures that whatever I need to achieve will not encroach on the freedom of others to choose the rules they live by.

Any wisdoms that I receive through this teaching and the connection therein will be used solely to inspire myself and others about a greater wisdom that exists.

I agree to this with complete acknowledgement and with the desire to understand the wisdoms of the fifth dimension.

In making this agreement, I ask that it be made known to me how I can put right any misguided teachings that I have unwittingly passed on to others prior to my conscious knowledge of the existence of a universal justice system.

This agreement is made with my conscious decision to apply this primary code of behaviour in all aspects of my life.

I accept with honour the responsibility of being a protector for the purity of the soul plane, and I look forward to the contentment of my heart, peace of mind, and well-being of my soul.

Say yes to this statement for your new journey to begin!

This protocol has spelt out the importance of your commitment, and of your belonging to something much bigger than you alone.

Step 3: Code of Conduct

Step three is a code of conduct attached to your commitment that you have just agreed to. These are your first guidelines to success that will help to keep you focused so you know you are on the right track. I have done this because I believe it is important to understand in a very real way how to start your journey that will be seen to be working for you. This calms the mind down so emotional intelligent thinking can take over. It is important for these rules to be observed, as they are all attached to the soul level of intelligence.

If I am to help you overcome previous teachings of behavioural responses, these guidelines will help you to understand a bit more and make sense of your intention to review your actions up until now. They have been written in a simple, logical format. Many have said these guidelines made total sense in helping them understand the first step in working *with* the soul plane as a joint venture to return the ultimate authority to the discretion of their souls with the guidance of universal law.

Turn the page to learn about step three of your initiation into your new belonging.

Everything you read is about keeping manners, morals, respect, and honour for your soul's worth as the highest priority for your own well-being. This is done to ensure that re-education of the senses can be achieved with the best chance of success.

There must be rules on behaviour before anything else. Following are a few basic standards on how to keep yourself in check when faced with adversity. I have designed the following to help with "first response" dilemmas.

Our Code of Conduct

- Always be attentive to your needs of maintaining harmony within the self and with others.
- Always act with kindness as the first response to another person.
- Honour another's point of view by acknowledging his or her feelings but being polite in response if you do not agree.
- If you feel a conflict of opinion, the person you are talking to is not a person you should be talking to. The moment it becomes heated, remove yourself from the situation and leave it to those who prefer noise to truth.
- Be dignified at all times in your manner. Respect starts with the self. Radiate this and you will treat others with the same level of respect.
- Arrogance gets in the way of anything good. Wisdom allows confidence to be quiet.
- Unconditional acceptance of another person opens every door.
- Do not be quick to judge others, or you will leave others to judge you with the same speed.
- If you cannot find a calm way to react, do not react.
- Sometimes you need time to assess the best response. Where possible, allow yourself this treasure. Do not allow yourself to be hurried into making a decision that does not feel right.
- Bullying, whether physical, emotional, or mental, is intolerable; "bullying" is an alternative word for abuse. The next time you want to get your own way, remember this.
- Know what to stand your ground over—and what not to.
- Seek wisdom in knowing when to keep quiet and when to speak (this is to protect you).
- All of this is leading you into how to think primarily from an alternative viewpoint when confronted with antagonism.
- When you have achieved this, it would be beneficial to show others how you did it too.

- Please remember that no soul would intentionally hurt another soul, because it is not in the soul's interest to do so.
- It is the misguided teachings of another person's soul that cause negative responses. We are all guilty of some form of manipulation at one point or another.
- Be mindful of cause and effect in all that you do from this moment on.

You have just completed the third stage of initiation!

This where it all becomes real! Be proud to belong to this new conscious, soul way of thinking, where time is used wisely.

8

THE WAY FORWARD

Now you can be proud to belong to something bigger! You have just taken a massive leap into the unknown. You have used *trust* on a very basic level, which will propel you forward into a new, confident you. Reread the universal law agreement and code of conduct regularly to remind you that you now belong to a universal community of sisters who have taken the step that you have just taken to increase your own self-awareness. Also review the pledge to help women take control of their natural position within the human race to bring about equality through harmony of the senses and an understanding of it right from the beginning, the way it should always have been.

I suggest you read the entire book first and then go back to this section, as answers to your own questions might be answered further on in the book.

Now that you have become part of the sisterhood, you will have access to all souls that have lived a life on earth and have now passed beyond the veil of physical sight. But if you need a question answered on helping you with your own life, you can tune in to the frequency of the soul plane and ask for help. Keep the symbol of the feminine protocol in sight by either putting it in a frame and looking at it or just holding it in your hand. Concentrate on this and ask for help in whatever you need. I can send to you an A4 or A5 picture along with your certificate request; just ask for this to be included. The same goes for the soul reiki symbol for men.

Know what it is you need help with. *Speak* of what you are having trouble with. The first port of call of emotional intelligence is identifying for yourself where the initial problem lies within your own experiences in life. You are then already opening a door to a higher frequency, as it will be acknowledged you are making the first step into knowing the area that you need help with.

This is true activation of your initiation, which is now with you for life anytime you request help. If you are able to, have a candle of your choosing next to your picture, and light it when you want to go into asking for help as you ask your question. This is merely to engage your feminine senses of tranquillity, but really you can do whatever is right for you. It might be that you like to go for a walk to clear your mind and be at one with nature. It might be when you are ironing or cooking that answers come to you. It might be when you are doing needlework or knitting. I hope you get my point. It's wherever you feel most at one with your inner self—that deep place that only you know is there.

Even the most horrific places in your mind can be reached by this new energy, brining you to question why you still carry this horror and to ask why you needed to go through that experience. This in itself is giving your pain a hand to hold so it can pull you out of *any* emotional trauma, allowing you to start to control your answer by applying emotional logic.

You will know when you have engaged in this field of the search for wisdom because it will activate a different part of your brain. When you start to find the true answer, you will feel a light bulb moment, and the trauma will be overtaken by intelligent logic; this is where knowledge meets wisdom and results in emotional integrity. This shows you the answer to *why*. A new freedom emerges as every time the habit of trauma surfaces, you create a new habit of calming it down by remembering you have already dealt with that one and got your answer. If a higher wisdom is trying to reach you, that will happen too. But never look at pain and blame. True wisdom leaves those emotions at the bottom, using them as a springboard to get you nearer to your soul, which holds all the answers that are trying to reach you.

Life becomes an adventure as you realize that you are the master of how you react and respond to situations and you can overcome your pain and use the wisdom that comes to you for yourself as you let go of past experiences. You will no longer have to carry on repeating the same cycle unless you choose to. But if you choose to, it will be because you have managed to turn around the feeling of control, to see how the situation benefits you, until you can change your future.

Wisdom allows the mind to be calm so you can see the truth of why you are in a situation you are in or why you had to experience what you have gone through or are going through to get you to another place. This is being in control of your own destiny, where you can *trust* in universal law, which is working with your soul to ensure only that those things that are necessary for you to experience will take place. If you have had enough of your present experience, ask to be pulled out and give all of your energy to the universe to do that. Know this is going to happen and then allow time for change to take place. It will. It is as loyal to you as you are to it. You will be heard.

You are an intelligent woman; you have just been abused regarding the right to show your intelligence in this way. You have never seen your own thoughts and feelings as intelligence. The important thing is to allow an answer to come to you! I explain it to those I teach like this: If you are not leaving your mind open for a response, how will you hear it? It's like knocking on the door and running away before anyone has a chance to open the door and let you in!

This does take time, so don't be alarmed or disappointed if you don't get a response immediately. Just be determined and committed and know exactly what your question is and why you need change to happen. The response will probably not be in physical language. It will be in a feeling of knowingness of the answer. It might also come to you through the hearing of a song that grabs your attention, perhaps through the words in the song. It could also occur through overheard conversations or something you read about. These are all frequencies used by the soul plane if you are keeping an open mind.

The important thing is to keep an open mind as to what you truly seek.

Before you start, you might also want to consider having some crystals with you to enhance your connection. If you are new to the crystal world, I suggest having a rose quartz and an amethyst crystal with you. Bond with them by thanking them for any help they can give to you in reaching answers to enhance your femininity and your connection to the soul plane that you have been missing. (I just put a small piece of whatever crystal feels right inside my bra, ladies!)

You can buy necklaces, bracelets, and the like. But a small piece of the crystal you choose won't cost more than a couple of pounds at most, for those that need to keep an eye on their budget. Just research on the Internet which crystal you need for help in answers by searching "crystals to help with [your issue]". These crystals are nice to have around the house at various points. They all add up to you increasing your feminine connection to your soul.

Crystals are used even in the highest of churches, cathedrals, and temples to enhance oneness. Did you know that? I have written more about crystals further on in this book to enlighten you on their unseen worth, in case you have never heard of their qualities.

I tell you now that you will be amazed at how crystals physically saved my life once! They have also on many occasions helped me to access the deeper subconscious and have been the go-between when my mind is under attack because the constant controlling forces in this world that live in our minds feel threatened by my insistence on finding a hidden truth! Crystals are living energy and do not judge.

There are other levels of the psyche where a more formal approach needs to be made. This is for those that cannot find, or "feel", at this moment in time, the thought of involving crystals. I say this because at the beginning of my journey, I had never heard of crystals and just didn't understand what they were all about. That's okay. We have all been brought up from a different start point of learning. The more removed from our core of knowing all things feminine we are, the less we see the point of introducing something that seemingly has no sense attached to it. I Know! I have been there to.

We all have different starting points. That's okay. There are many warriors needed for our cause. You are bringing your own unique gifts to the table. But the true feminine warrior hears all before passing judgement. You have all the time in the world to get to know your role in this quest of leading your family out of apathy and into true knowing. You cannot pass on valid wisdoms if you don't know all the facts, can you?

I'll now return to the point of reaching out from your inner sense to the inner sense of the fifth dimension, for those that are very practical in their approach to life but feel there is something that they need to learn about to safeguard the future generations of their family line.

I always play calming music to settle my senses if I feel out of balance. One can't hear the right communication if one is anxious and not in a good place. Having said that, if you need to be pulled out of a bad emotional place, another method you can try—especially if you are generally scientific in your approach to life and are finding it hard to adjust to the feminine angle just yet—is to call on universal law and see yourself in a courtroom and bowing down to the deliberation of the wisdom of the court as a matter of respect. State your problem and ask for an answer to be found that will stop the destructive thoughts towards yourself and others that are causing you harm. Then let go of the outcome. You have just passed your problem to the highest minds and to the soul plane for them to protect you, which means you can feel calm again in knowing you have done the right thing. The answer to your problem was beyond you to find, so you have passed it to those that can help. You will get your answer. But your part to play is to totally let go of the drama of the situation.

Here is another way of looking at the subject of awkward discussions, which was covered earlier in the book. This may be a simpler version to remember.

If you hold on to the drama, universal law cannot interact, as you are blocking its intervention by keeping hold of it. The logic of this is simple. Look at it like this: if you are still holding all the ingredients to a cake, how can anyone else make it?

What you find and feel is right usually is right. Give it three days to reach you from the soul plane. (That's how long it can take for the wholeness of the message to be fully understood.) Concentrate your mind on finding the highest answer to help you and to achieve good for all. As you get used to asking for help in this way, the length of time it takes to receive an answer can be shortened to just hours or even minutes.

Keep the answers in high regard and with respect for all those who have spent their entire lives, in most cases, not being heard. Always say thank you for the help you receive. After all, you would want someone to say thank you to you if you helped them, wouldn't you? Gratitude is a great gift to give and receive.

Okay, I have just explained how to access the inner levels of the psyche that are there for us all to access.

What also may be something to keep in mind is this: For the true believer, mistakes never happen; there are just unexpected possibilities that surface, which in time will increase one's wisdom. The universe sees all and will always let you learn by way of a method that you find works for you. As you get used to recognizing the clues, your ability to speed up your learning capacity will increase.

9

MY SPIRITUAL GROWTH TIMELINE

Now I think the time is right for me to return to 1994, when I started this journey of self-assessment and reflection. One thing I do want to make abundantly clear is that I would not ask you to do something I have not done or would not be willing to do myself. I am a hands-on teacher. I walk beside all of my students (that's what you are now) in companionship and harmony.

My experiences, and those of all of my students over the past twenty-five years plus, have been put into the pot to help you and be there for you. When you enter a state of oneness within yourself, you have access to information, as I have described. What with that and the entire soul plane, you will not fail to find answers that will enhance your emotional well-being. And there is so much more that I still have to tell you!

To follow is the timeline of events that have been my "working" life—that of leaving my life in the hands of the universe, consciously, to open and shut doors on the levels of a different type of awareness. I hope this aspect of me will inspire confidence regarding what is available when you truly believe in your worth and realize that there is hidden knowledge that needs to surface, according to your own beliefs on the purpose of why you are here.

Whatever drove you to believe in my words, you have created a new you in that process, and that new you is waiting for you to command your disciplines and actions. You are now your own person, with a renewed sense of being. You have a set of moral guidelines and principles that hadn't been spelt out for you with the clarity that you now have. You can now start to make your life work for you and with you; you can make all conscious decisions on your actions and reactions.

To believe you are worth it, and to begin to change the story of you, what I suggest is that you write your own journal of your own experiences and how you dealt with them. This will be part of your legacy to leave for your children and future generations to come.

To break the intensity of the teaching, I will take you back to the beginning of *my* new world, ladies—that night in 1994. I continue to share various aspects for you to know in the hope that it helps you to have more faith in yourself and your abilities. if you do have strong, new thoughts in your mind, it's okay; that is normal. This is all to inspire you, to help you to read between the lines for hidden guidance and messages.

When I felt that hand on my forehead and saw the oriental gentleman sitting beside me, I had no idea what it meant. But I remember with absolute clarity that it happened.

I started to judge my behaviour, and I soon understood that what I was doing was wrong, mainly regarding my attitude to men and sex. Gradually I returned to my status of honour and self-respect, and I became more spiritual in my manner as I let go of the earthly attitude that I had been taught regarding my purpose here as far as men were concerned. As I found my own worth as a woman and a mother, something happened to me.

I started to hear communications in my mind that felt warm and loving. I felt that I was here for a reason, but I did not know at that time the full extent of that reason. I began to get the feeling that I was bringing masters that were in charge of our well-being on earth a new insight as to the plight of women. It felt as though they were curious to the point of having no idea what it was like for women on this earthly plane. I felt as though I was forming an agreement with them that would teach them what they needed to know. It all felt as though I knew exactly what was going on, and I agreed to it.

After three years of this communication, in 1997, I suddenly felt an urge to start an organization to help women to understand what I knew, so they could know also. It was the precursor of what I am doing now for you. It did not last; I had not got the experience that I needed to reach women in a way in which I could be properly heard. So I went back to the drawing board, wondering what I was doing wrong. Why couldn't most people see what I had to offer? I soon realized that only I could see it, feel it, and be it. There were levels of comprehension I needed to go over to learn how to talk to people in a language they could understand.

It was now 2001, and I was having a burning sensation in my chest that was prompting me to go to Egypt and stand in front of the Sphinx. All I knew was that it had something to do with my father, who had passed some five years previously. I hadn't even got a passport at this point, and I had hardly been out of the country. This burning desire became so strong that I knew I had to make it happen. I was willing to sell my car if I had to, but I had to go. As it happened, I managed to get a credit card, and I booked the trip as soon as the card came through.

On arrival in Cairo at around 1:00 a.m., we were told by the travel guide that we had to be up and ready to leave at 5:00 a.m. to go to our planned trip to the pyramids and Sphinx. About ten minutes after going to bed, I was awoken by a large white humanoid shape standing beside me. I was so tired that I said, "Look, if you have something to tell me that I need to know, can you find a way of me hearing it? I am so tired I am going to turn over and go to sleep." I felt no fear. It all felt normal to me.

When I got to the Sphinx, I just stood in front of it and cried. I had reached the point I needed to reach, and I felt I had done what had been asked of me. To this day, all I know was that it was meaningful. I have never looked back, and my wisdom and spiritual growth have no bounds. I also know my father is with me always.

Since that first time, I have visited Egypt many times, to learn of ancient ways. I suppose it is also apparent to me that they followed the rules that I speak to you of. Ancient Egyptians believed that one's heart was weighed against a feather to see whether one was carrying the baggage of a guilty heart. If that was the case, one was eaten by a monster.

If one's heart was light, equal to the feather, one would go through to an amazing afterlife. I have followed up the teachings of Thoth (the emerald tablets) and found them to be very true to my own understanding of life I have arrived at with the guidance I have been, and am still being, given. I do believe he, too, is with me and guiding me to help teach the unspoken language of the soul that rules our core well-being.

One other thing that was apparent in my constant search for the truth of where it all went wrong was the fact that corruption was happening even then, before the time of religion as we know it. The temple priests devised a system whereby any wealthy Egyptians could buy their way out of having their soul weighed in truth by having a shabti doll buried with them that would take any punishment that was to be coming their way.

So as I said, there was corruption even then. Much can be learned by looking into the past and reading between the lines of the most learned writings. Look in the right way, and the answer to anything can be found. It is all down to the intention of your search for knowledge.

In 2000, I felt a knowing that I needed to go to Crete because there was something important that I needed to do there. My instincts told me there was *someone* that desperately needed my help. That is all I knew.

As I arrived at the hotel, I was greeted by someone I had met on a previous visit. She told me she had met someone she really liked, but he had problems dealing with problems stemming from having been in combat, as he was a veteran of the Vietnam War. She said that it came to a head when there was a firework display on locally and he ran inside and hid under the bed, putting his head in his hands. She had to coax him out and hold him close to her, as he couldn't cope with the noise of the bangers.

So I met her new friend and observed the inner core of him,

without him knowing what I was doing. It was a pleasant introduction, and he seemed fine on the surface.

I then spent the week I was there entering realms that no one goes to, to find what the problem really was. And I found it. On my last day there, I waited in the lounge of the hotel, where I had asked my new friend to meet me before I left for the airport. I started chatting to him about his time in Vietnam. He began getting agitated, mainly because of where I was asking him to go. I gave him a clue as to what I had found, so he could fill in the gaps. I said to him, "I know that while you were out there, you overstepped a mark, didn't you?"

At this he broke down and cried. He told me that he was in charge of his soldiers, and whilst going through the jungle, they came across a village. Whilst there, they saw a young girl who was not armed. He said that the soldiers shot and killed her when there was no need, and he did not stop them, although he could have done so.

Whatever happened in that moment, I knew it was because he had overstepped his own moral code on behaviour. It had got entwined with his honour, and he couldn't get out of this emotional turmoil, even after twenty-five years. I held him and told him secret information he needed to hear. He calmed down and thanked me profusely.

He said many soldiers live in the trees in parks because they can't get over things that happened. There is no more for me to explain here that you to need to know, apart from what is possible with the healing power of the fifth dimension through my techniques and the teaching you will learn about. My mission accomplished, I left for the airport to come back to England.

I have since counselled many soldiers returning from active service who cannot find peace of mind for myriad different reasons. They all find peace with the words I speak and the healing available. They all have to agree (and do, willingly) with the universal law agreement.

I share with you my research so that it will help you to understand that meddling with the purity of the soul and its worth never wins; it cannot. Man can short circuit the system for self-gain, but the truth will always surface at some point and be used for those who are looking for true answers because the truth, as described herein, does not ring true.

I hadn't got the finer communication skills that I needed to communicate. I needed more training, as well as more experiences, both spiritual and earthly. But I never doubted my path. That was set in stone. I am here to help women gain access to the information that I have, so I set about doing that on a totally different level. This required total trust, as the physical words that I had got used to hearing were now reduced to intuition and feelings.

I had to become one with women again, on a very real level. I had got used to living amongst masters of another realm where wisdom rules everything. As my trust grew, I was tested. So many things happened to me. I was thought to have cancer in my liver. Scans showed a patch of shadows. My strength of trust kept me going. On further investigation, it wasn't cancer; it mimicked cancer, though. It turned out to be something harmless.

A few years went by, and whilst investigations were happening as I felt an uncomfortable feeling in my stomach, and after hospital scans, it was suspected I had a large cancerous growth the size of a melon. The scan showed it quite clearly. Surgery was booked very quickly. It turned out to be tissue—nothing cancerous.

My faith wouldn't allow me to fear—ever. In fact, whilst I was in hospital, I was going around talking to other women patients, giving them comfort by seeing their problem and explaining to them how to address it. I appeared to be able to look into their bodies and describe what I could see. This was a new ability to me.

I continued to grow in trust and learning, and I created a path that meant following my instinct and intuition to keep open the portal of connectivity to the masters of this higher authority of universal law and the seat of the soul. I was sent on many missions, which I had to fund myself, but the money was always made available one way or another. I have been sent to many parts of the world where I have had chance meetings with people that started telling me of their personal emotional concerns and needed to hear something I could tell them to alleviate their troubled minds.

I have travelled far and wide, my wisdom growing with each encounter. My gifts of sight into the human body, the emotional field, the very core of existence, and beyond never leave me unsatisfied.

In early 2004 (ten years into my training from the netherworlds), I had an urge to travel around Thailand. I knew only that I needed to go to the River Kwai in Kanchanaburi, which the Second World War film *Bridge on the River Kwai* had been made about. I didn't know why I was having to go there (as was always the case); I knew only that I did. My three-week tour around Thailand took me to some exquisite places, where I learnt new wisdoms on many levels.

Eventually I arrived at the hotel that stands on the ground where the concentration camp was for those captured by the Japanese, who were made to build the bridge across the river. I looked around and was told that a sleeping hut for prisoners of war was still there, and I was allowed to go inside the small circular building made mainly out of bamboo.

As I stood inside, I mentally asked whether there was anything I needed to hear to help me understand why I was there. A resounding word loudly echoed inside my head. It was "camaraderie". At that moment, I instantly understood what that meant. It meant that no matter what had to be endured, their spiritual brotherhood kept them all going in a oneness that only they could have felt and known.

It was the perfect message, and I felt it too. I felt all that they went through, but their togetherness in their pain was everything. Their comradery was such that they could not be broken in spirit—the link to their souls. I thanked them for their words and emotions that I was privy to in that moment.

If you have not seen the film, it is well worth watching.

The one thing that I knew deep down was that corruption, along with the misguidance corruption manifests, was a ruling factor on earth. For far too long, no one has known the truth of how to live in a conscience-free way. Everyone is troubled by something. What would it take for me to rid myself of this dark matter I had collected along the way of my training?

As it happened, in 2005 I had an opportunity to go to Uluru—or

Ayers Rock, as it is commonly known—in Australia. I just knew I had to go there. Upon my arrival, I asked a local shopkeeper how I could speak to the tribal elders of the Aboriginal tribe that lives there. (Words come out of my mouth without me knowing where they come from sometimes!)

The shopkeeper laughed at me, saying, "No one goes in there! Their encampment is protected, and there is punishment of imprisonment for anyone who attempts it."

I said, "OK, but I don't understand." I needed to go in there and talk to someone. I was asked to leave my phone number with the shop owner and was told someone might ring me.

Within an hour, I had a phone call from someone called Bob Randell. He said his sons were coming to town the following morning, and he asked me to wait in the car park for a white four-by-four at 11:00 a.m. I did this without hesitation, not knowing what was coming next. All I knew was that my instincts told me I could let go of all of the pent-up horror that I held in my mind regarding the corruption of the teaching of this world, and I let it go once I was inside. As it turned out, this was another misconception of why I was there.

Whilst on the journey inside the white four-by-four, I learned from these two charming boys of Bob Randell what life was like inside their sacred camp. It was a disappointing horror story. I was told of alcohol abuse, drug abuse, and a widespread lack of a feeling of purpose. When I reached the destination of their home, Bob came out to greet me.

Bob was, in fact, an elder of the tribe, and as it turned out, he was famous for his attempts to get the world to understand the plight of children stolen when white men came to their encampment and changed the way things were for them. He was taken whilst in the woods, put in a mission, and brought up by missionaries, who taught him what he was told was the right way to behave.

The missionaries knew nothing of life as he had been taught— of being connected to the earth and knowing earth magic and the harmony between nature and man. He was not the only child that was taken. Many of them were. Their only crime was their having gone around as nature intended, without clothes on. This caused them to be seen as savages, and for this they were taken away and sent to missionaries to be brought up by them, in a 'civilised' society.

These children had come about by their mothers having got pregnant by the white explorers who "found" them. They decided it wasn't right for the children of these liaisons to be brought up in their natural habitat of the aboriginal villages with their mothers. Hence the story of them is well known and well documented today. Bob himself was always travelling the world with his sons, singing about their plight and the injustice they had to endure. He did not know how old he was.

I was there for quite a few hours, and whilst I was there, it rained on the rock. Bob's son shouted for us to go out and have a look, as it is a rare occasion and happens only as an omen that something important is happening at that moment. They both took it to mean that my presence that day was the thing being honoured.

Bob took me back to my hotel in the evening. Whilst on our journey back, he said I was there for a reason. He also said he knew that when the time was right, I would go back and help his people get the retribution that was justifiable as to the continued raping of their rights. I understood that the Aboriginals had been tricked into signing away their land rights so they got only 5 percent of their land rights for tourism and the like.

I remember thinking to myself, "That's not what I deal with; I am here for soul wrongdoings"—and this most certainly came under that category. The young Aboriginal men were a sad copy of who their ancestors were. They had been corrupted by social security money—"free" money. This was something they had never had before, and it was offered to them for the small price of a signature on a piece of paper that gave away their rights to their land. They had sold their souls' worth for money. That seems a familiar story, worldwide, on some level.

Anyway, back to the journey to my hotel. The guards of the hotel came rushing up to the car as soon as Bob pulled up to warn him off.

He put his hands up and told them, "I am only dropping the lady off." This was 2005.

Bob phoned about a year later to say he was coming to England and we could meet up, but as it turned out I had booked a holiday and was not able to see him then. I tried to contact him later, but he passed away the month before I phoned. I still believe that meeting was meant to be. That afternoon saw lots of anguish being released and heard.

Maybe his plight was heard in a way that it hadn't been before by those that listened through me—through the Court of Universal Justice, specifically—to hear stories of conscious wrongdoing by those who use their power of financial influence in exchange for the worth of soul gratification, which, once done, is a hard journey to come from. It is not impossible, I should add. It just takes determination to put things right from the right perspective and not let history repeat itself in the same way—which is what this book is all about: natural retribution from the highest authority known to the soul of man.

Another poignant moment for me was at the top of Mount Sinai in Egypt. We started the climb to the top at 2:00 a.m. It was such a magical experience. Whilst climbing, I counted eight shooting stars that crossed over my path. I felt so at one with the universe and thanked each one of them for the natural excitement and cosmic energy I was being infused with. We got to the top just before dawn, and as the sun came up, I saw something I couldn't explain. I said in my head, "What is this I am seeing?" I was told to relax my eyes. As I did, I saw what I can only describe as white dots darting around the way flies do, with quick, angled movements.

The feeling was one of excitement from them. I was then told that what I was seeing was spiritual DNA and they were my army to help me bring about change in the world. This was amazing for me! But how was I to do that? There was still a long way to go. I couldn't feel the link to other women generally, and I instinctively knew this was showing me that I was on the right path and that patience and tolerance still needed to rule my senses. But I also knew that when the time was right, I would *feel* their presence again, and we could go to work together on this massive quest I had undertaken. This was just before Christmas 2009.

The other poignant thing I want to tell you about was that 2007 found me being a landlord of a pub for a while and having to experience a lot of situations crammed into my life in a short space of time. This lasted for around a year. It was obviously necessary for my training that I go through all the horrors of being immersed in a world that was the opposite extreme of what my persona would choose.

I learned hard and fast about the various characters that came through the doors. Few were there for just a friendly chat and to pass the time of day. Most had emotional hang-ups. I could have spent my life trying to help every soul there, but it would have only drained my energy, as no one really wanted to *learn* about how to evolve.

Most were in a continual state of apathy, just trying to glean momentary understanding, but did not have the will to change. The alcohol persuasion was too much of a contender for their minds to take on. It was exhausting. Literally a year went by, practically to the day, and the pub was shut by the brewery overnight, as they wanted to sell it for the land it was on.

There were, as I said, some very harsh lessons that I needed to chalk up as personal experiences to be able to cover a lot more of those that are controlled by habits—no matter what those habits are. So once again, I searched for the wisdom. The whole aspect of that year of learning whilst being a landlady and working eighty-four hours a week found my health appearing to be decidedly bad, as the hospital did tests and told me they had found a shadow on my liver and it didn't look good

I knew that if their suspicions were founded, it was something I needed to go through. As it turned out, a more intense investigatory procedure was carried out, and it was determined that the shadow was extra blood vessels within the liver structure; it was not a life-threatening condition. I understood their words with a wisdom that made sense to me only.

Whilst I was still a pub landlady, I felt as though I needed to clear myself of all the adverse energy that my body and spirit were having to handle by being in this position, so when I noticed an advert for a four-day holiday in Rome living in a convent just outside St Peters Square (home of the pope), I booked it and went.

This holiday was just what I needed, and it provided yet more proof through the experiences I encountered there, which I would never have had if I had not run with my intuition that I needed this timeout. I stayed in a simple room without any TV or radio (I suppose obviously so), and I took a book to read on all the great masters that have had a following (Carl Jung, Buddha, and Christ, to name but a few), which was most enlightening. I ate the simple, nourishing meals with monks, priests, and sisters that shared a life within the boundaries of the Catholic faith, in a building opposite the convent.

I went into Vatican City to look around the church there, and I experienced something I was not expecting. I went into a local shop, and there was a lady in front of me and a man in front of her, being served. After a minute or so of queuing, another man walked into the shop. The man at the front of the queue finished buying his purchase, and as the lady in front stepped up to the counter, the shopkeeper looked straight past both of us and served the man who had just walked into the shop.

I thought this very odd and couldn't at first get my head around what had just happened. The same thing then happened in a cafe, where I entered the premises first, but a man walking in a few steps behind me got shown to a table and I was left until he had been seated. Then I went into another shop, and the same thing happened again. By this time the penny dropped and I realized that women have no status other than to come last anywhere inside Vatican City, the place where religion is at its holiest.

I was livid. I went back to the convent, incensed at this, and asked one of the sisters there if she could arrange for me to have a one-to-one with the pope, as I needed to sort this unacceptable situation out. As I saw it, he was her boss, and I needed to speak to him. She was horrified at my request for an audience. I would say she was in her late sixties and had lived there all of her life, yet she had never met him. Thinking back now, I realize that of course she wouldn't have.

So on the Sunday morning, I heard from a fellow "inmate" that the pope came out onto the balcony on Sunday mornings to bless the crowd. I felt the urge to go, to observe, and learn something that needed to be known. I didn't know what it would be; I just knew this was an opportunity that had presented itself—the very fact that I was there on a Sunday and this was happening.

I walked down into Vatican City, and into St. Peter's Square, where the people were massing in huge numbers. The pope came out onto the balcony and started his sermon. I felt agitated. This was not the reason I was there. Something didn't feel right about this. There was something else that I needed to understand and find as to the *true* reason I was there. I looked around me.

There wasn't a space anywhere; everyone was so closely packed together. I felt even more agitated as the prayers started to take place and everyone had their heads down. What *was* it I was there for? My head lowered in prayer mode, I was darting my eyes first to the left, and then to the right. Then I snapped my head back to the left, where I saw the feminine energy of an obelisk representing the power of Isis, goddess of Egypt. it. It beckoned me like a beacon. It was standing there, towering right in the middle of the square, in plain sight.

I knew I needed to go to it, so I weaved my way to it, passing a few people at a time, trying not to get noticed too much for what I was doing in the middle of prayer time, which would not have looked good. When I got there, there was another problem. My instinct was telling me that I needed to hug the obelisk. But there was a problem. There was a metal fence around it, stopping anyone from walking up to it, as well as Italian police guarding its perimeter.

I went straight up to one of the guards and said to him, "Do you speak English?"

He replied, "Yes."

I said to him, "I really want to touch the obelisk; do you mind if I climb over the fence and do that?"

He looked puzzled and awkward, but I just looked into his eyes with a look of determination and pleading at the same time. He said, "OK."

I lunged my bag his way, asking him if he could look after it whilst I climbed over the fence, thanking him for allowing me to do this, as simultaneously other police swarmed in on me to stop me; but he put his hand up to stop them, speaking in Italian, and they all backed off. I went up to the obelisk, put my arms around it, and shut my eyes to absorb its energy, feminine to feminine.

Unfortunately for me, there was a marble-type covering surrounding the base, but I put my mind beyond that so I could experience the ancient energy of the obelisk. One may wonder exactly *why* this obelisk is where it is. I am sure there are many explanations, but my own intuition is enough to know whose energy it is sapping up.

This task now complete, I went back to my room at the convent, where many things started to make sense to me as I went over the various incidents I had encountered on that trip. As always, the wisdoms just keep on growing, the understandings growing wider and fuller as to further prove that my original "cause and effect" reasoning was still right.

So, to sum up, I got the well-needed respite from being a pub landlady, and I learned so much about how women are still generally treated in the most revered of cities. But I must mention my gratitude again for the policeman that allowed me to do the unthinkable. He must have been in touch with his feminine side for that moment; the masters were at work when I needed them. It never fails that I am left in awe at and forever grateful for the intervention of the power, intertwined with harmony, of the fifth dimension, where things always happen exactly when they need to, when one's belief and faith rule all other senses.

In 2010, I was ready to open up a teaching centre with a shop to sell all things spiritual and do readings. I was really excited at this prospect. I signed the contract on an amazing property to rent. It was a large converted barn with living accommodation upstairs and a large open-plan space for me downstairs. At last (so I thought) I could make my living out of what I love to do—helping people find their own connection. I just love that feeling when they connect for the first time. Words cannot express the lifting of spirit that they encounter.

Anyway, as you have probably guessed, nope—it wasn't time. As I said, I signed the contract, and it was mine from that very moment. Not an hour went by before I had a phone call from a dear friend telling me she had just received test results from the doctor stating she was well into the third stage of ovarian cancer. I dropped all my plans and was determined to see this through with her. I was convinced I could find a way to cure her. I don't know why, but it just seemed a logical continuation of where my knowledge could take me.

So instead of opening up the shop, I moved in and started to research the physical body connection of the fifth-dimension way of seeing things. The building was right in the middle of the countryside, with a few other buildings there—all converted barns. I couldn't have wanted a better place to be than here for deeper research to take place. I found I could now talk to trees, and they talked back! Does that sound ridiculous?

I used to be a mortgage broker at one time, and now I can liaise with nature. It is all a matter of tuning into a certain frequency. I had no idea my abilities had grown so much. I researched, and I bought books that took me into ancient worlds. I read up on T-cells; I read everything I could find from the medical world. Mary was told she had around eighteen months if she was lucky.

I was having none of that. I went within with all that I had gleaned knowledge of, asking for the guidance to allow me the ability to find answers of this disease and reverse it, stop it, and find a different outcome. I carried on researching and started writing at the same time. Not only was I finding answers for my friend; I was finding the need to write about *all* of my findings on loads of subjects that I had covered since 1994.

I wrote of all of my knowledge—all of my experiences. I had always written things, but it always felt as though I was writing speeches that I would be giving to women who wanted to hear my words. Back in 1997, I saw visions of me going into a well-packed hall, with people eagerly awaiting my attendance to hear me speak on stage. Then I would be leaving that venue and going on to the next. More recently, I had a vision of being in America, all glamourous and glitzy. In this vision, I was in a massive auditorium, and it had the word "she" in lights above the stage. I entered, but I was also at the back of the auditorium, watching my entrance onto the stage. I looked different, but I think this was a realization in the vision that I would be changing into someone I hardly recognized, and this I had to do to ensure my words continued on their journey across the globe.

Anyway, back to my friend Mary and my writing and research on disease. I pushed my boundaries daily, and suddenly, after about four months, I found myself being able to talk to her body and the cells within it. I spoke to them and discussed a strategy for the blockages to be dealt with. I understood that it was, as I had suspected, emotion that had caused this disease to take a hold on her body.

I learned that this was the message her soul was trying to get through to her to stop her ways of putting others before herself. I negotiated with her body, having to decipher the language with which it spoke to me.

I agreed that things would change. I gave a way out for the disharmony to leave, allowing a flow of energy to occur where the blockages were. Mary had already had an operation scheduled to remove most of her stomach because of the spread of the cancer, and she was to have a colostomy bag fitted at the same time.

I started giving her my own form of treatment using reiki energy along with my enhanced knowledge and frequency setting. I could see inside of her body and calmed down the energy within. She managed to fit in two treatments (she was a very busy lady and was not going to let cancer get in her way) from me before surgery.

When the doctors performed the surgery, they could not believe what they found. The cancer had shrunk to such a degree that they just had to remove what they could from the ovaries; her stomach was, for the most part, left intact. Mary said she knows it was my treatments that made this happen, although she was undergoing hospital chemotherapy at the same time, and the doctors put her miraculous turnaround down to this.

I explained to Mary that she would have to abide by the new instruction that I had given her on her lifestyle and what needed to be done to ensure that we could rid her body of the cancer totally. Unfortunately, Mary could not do that, and her situation got worse. But I did keep her going for another eight years after that.

She became well known for being treated with experimental drugs, because she could cope with it, and her picture and story were published in the hospital magazine at one point to promote the possibilities of recovery with the hospital treatments she received. I have contacted various cancer charities, offering my services to women, but no one wants to know about "natural" treatments. I wonder why? I will leave you to your own thoughts on that.

Mary asked for treatments when her pain was really bad. She would be racked with pain when I entered her home but would be smiling when I left. She said something to me on one of my visits when she was particularly bad that will always encourage me to carry on doing what I do. I had just finished her treatment and was waiting for her to resurface from the deep levels of consciousness that I took her to, and she said to me, "Oh, Annette, there are so many women that need you." I have never forgotten her words, as they were spoken with such heartfelt sincerity. I burst out crying because I could feel in her the recognition of my capabilities.

She would not let me see her during the final weeks of her life, but she did phone me from hospital a couple of days before she passed. I did not know how bad she really was, because her spirit remained in tune with her soul. I said I would go up to the hospital and give her a treatment there, but she declined, saying that because of the possible contamination of germs, etc., I shouldn't go, as it might harm her.

I got a call from her best and closest friend two days later saying she had passed. I was in total shock. I couldn't stop crying all day. I couldn't understand why she would not let me save her.

After her funeral—which, as it happened, I could not attend

(meant to be)—I received a message from her through the channel of the fifth dimension that I could not see, because I believed I had failed her and my senses were distorted. Mary had been known to be a champion in putting herself forward for experimental treatments. What I couldn't see was that she was doing it from a *soul* perspective to *prove* that medicine was not the way forward. She was such a brave lady in the face of adversity. Mary believed so much in my work that she was willing to sacrifice her life for a world that would never understand this truth. But I do understand it, and she will be forever remembered by anyone reading this too. Mary will always be a go-between for anyone wanting to have healing from me of a physical nature to help with disease or disharmony of the senses when all else fails. Reconnection to the soul through the fifth dimension is a physical must as soon as possible. And I know this is possible for sure only because of my experiences with Mary.

She chose not to be saved. It was this that took her life. The drugs overruled her senses, and in a weakened state, they won, but she chose this and consciously acknowledged she did not want to maintain the fight, as it was too much to bear. She encountered her own spiritual war on a very real basis, but enough was enough, and forty-eight hours later, she passed, having made her decision. My natural treatments, which were not physically invasive, were what really counted. They kept her going. It would appear that although I could work with the experiments that were going on within her, the drugs could *not* work with me. This is the highest truth and the real truth of her end-of-life story.

Mary works with me from beyond the grave and is there to help me continue with my work. For those willing to learn a new language, that of the soul, recovery is possible. She will be there waiting in the fifth dimension to offer a helping hand. Mary follows a long line of women that have shown such bravery for no seen recognition. Her sacrifice needs to be remembered by all those I am able to help in the future in the way of treatments and guidance, where she resides, ready to give any woman the extra support and strength that are necessary when facing trauma of this scale.

This memory also reminds me of my business colleague and dear friend Colin. He believed in my passion to start up something to help women. He had previously seen first-hand my ability to make things happen on a working scale and supported me in my endeavours to move things along. In 1997, he was in hospital waiting to undergo tests and surgery for cancer.

I went to see him one evening before further surgery was to take place. The following day, he phoned me and explained that during the night, he was in terrible pain and he had a blood clot in his heart. The doctor told him he must lie completely still to enable him to perform the necessary procedure.

Colin says he was in a total state of panic and was finding it impossible to do that. He told me that suddenly I appeared, in his description, as a fairy on top of the curtain surrounding the bed, watching him, and he just stared at me. He says his body went completely calm and the doctor was able to do what was needed to his heart surgically. Colin told me that he was convinced I saved his life that night. As it turned out, the cancer had turned into leukaemia, and he had a life expectancy of two to five years. Colin lived for a further fifteen years.

It was 2016 when I received my final proof that this world was presently teaching from the wrong level of healing, and I had no idea this was coming. I could not have learned this in any other way to understand it in such an unexpected reversal of the experience I was setting out to have.

In March of that year, I was listening to the radio when the presenters were talking about the fact that it was International Women's Day. They were asking callers to phone in to say what they were doing to celebrate this. Before I knew what I was doing, I phoned up the number given, and said that I had an amazing way of teaching women how to be strong and would change their lives.

I didn't know it, but I had gone live on air, I believe, as the male commentator said, "Well that's good, but this is not the place to talk about that." That set me to thinking. The frequency of my senses continued to interact with my intuition, and it set my mind to working, considering what other means of communication could really have an impact. My mind went to an email I had received about an upcoming show at Alexandra Palace—a mind, body and soul exhibition. I contacted them and arranged to have a stall there in October.

I had got experience doing shows of this scale whilst being a mortgage broker, so the physicality of doing something like this did not faze me. But I soon realized that I couldn't explain everything I needed to in one hit. At this point, to be fair, I didn't even really know what I was doing there, apart from increasing my name awareness, so I waited for intuition to kick in and provide a thought pattern as to my purpose that could be seen in a business attitude on my reason for attendance.

Literally whilst setting up the stall, I devised a plan that I would offer dinner party talks. Some wanted me to talk at their yoga sessions or work environment settings, and it was all being received extremely well, and I felt it was the right approach. My girls were with me, and we all took the email addresses of those interested in booking, to get back to them at a later date.

I also booked a thirty-minute or so slot to explain what the feminine protocol is all about in a room provided. It was very difficult to explain in such a short while what my work is about, but I settled on a particular avenue of relationship-building with partners, as a lot of women attend the shows with that aspect in mind for readings and the like, as I understand it.

It did not go down well with a couple of women, who walked out of my seminar. On the balance of that, a young lady came to find me in my stall with tears in her eyes, saying what I had said hit a nerve with her, and she thanked me for the work I was doing. This is why I say this isn't for everyone to understand on the first approach. There is *so much* that I can tell you; it is multilayered and multidimensional. Learn all there is to know about the feminine protocol and you won't be disappointed. It does involve *every woman* at some point in her life, but now might not be the time for *every* woman. Because my work, my purpose, is so multifaceted, I couldn't get across the message the two ladies that left my talk early needed to hear in the limited time given. But this was just me sharing a side of realization (which was very helpful to most there). The *real* reason of my instinctual knowing that I had to be there, though, didn't come to me whilst at the show.

Amongst the other stallholders advertising their businesses were clairvoyants, life coaches, reiki healers, and spiritual advisors, some of which came up to me and talked about their businesses and shared with me about their experiences of working, which seemed to be generally not going the way it could.

It was only in hindsight that I collated all of this information because I felt something wasn't right; it seemed that I had missed something. My mind went over the three-day event, and I relived my conversations with all the wonderful ladies I had met who were eager to have me at one of their personal venues to talk some more. I remembered all of the different life coaches, healers, spiritual guides—men and women—and what they had opened up to me about regarding their work.

Then it hit me. They were *all* saying the same thing to me, but they were saying it in different guises. They felt that something was missing. They couldn't explain what it was. There seemed to be a block on their going further with their work, as they saw it, but they didn't know how to remove that block. I am speaking here of professional people whom I admire and respect for the work they do.

But this was the *proof* that I needed to hear on a soul level to know that the *teaching* they received for their qualifications was not coming from the highest level. When I relived the meeting of each one, in an honesty and truth that only I would know about, I could *feel* that the healing, logical frequency that deals with a truth that can unlock *any* emotional problem was not being used by them. Remember: as I have stated so many times before, this is not their fault. They have all received their qualifications from a system that does not involve going into the truth of our instinctual spiritual DNA which exists, telling us that something is not right. The reason they were bothered was because they were observing a truth that they couldn't explain, because they wanted the best for their clients. On the subconscious level, there was nowhere for them to go, so they were professionally imploding.

As it happened, on another note, I was unable to find all of the paperwork with the email addresses of those ladies that wanted me to attend their homes. I want to apologize for that here, as I have not had an opportunity to do that until now! It is four years on, and I would be happy to do that now that I have finished my training; and the masters from the metaphysical world would now not object, as I have completed my training to their satisfaction.

This was just another point in getting me to remember that I will be allowed to do only what is needed to be done, in the right order of things. I needed more research, a better understanding, the opening up of each point, and the understanding of wisdom, as well as the language to express my knowledge when the time came, to its fullest capability.

To enable this, I needed further personal proof from others that were in the profession of healing and caring for souls in need, and it was obviously time to do some hands-on research and receive some experience on a real, everyday level of the lives of people that needed extra support to live. I also needed to earn some money, as doing the show was expensive; and as it was clearly not the time for me to conclude my understandings yet (thanks for that), a job came my way almost immediately to earn money as a carer for those needing physical support.

I felt this was the right thing to do; my intuition and instinct told me so. It was just my ego I needed to adjust—not because I thought I was too good to do the work (far from it), but because standing in front of the public with that feeling of emotional control requires a skill that takes one outside of the private domain and into a public one, and a different skill set is required.

I had learned to go with the flow of what was required. And in truth, I have added that here only to bring about a conscious awareness in you, the reader, of the fact that all things, all experiences, are necessary; otherwise you would not be going through them on this level of integrity. But I still had to face myself with the actual *doing* of the physical work. This doesn't work if you cheat and do not become the person (even for a short while) that you need to be whilst in the employ of those that you are responsible to and that pay your wages.

There was also a certain freedom for me for a while whilst doing this job. I was looking after the person I had been assigned to whilst I was there. After leaving the person's home, I was free to be me, no longer responsible for the world's teaching for a while! It was akin to a respite, which I sorely needed, as the intensity of the wisdom I had obtained was reaching the point of imploding on itself.

I had reached by my own understanding, the knowledge that had been imparted to me at the very inception of my learning, that God / the soul plane / the real truth of life had been captured by man's misunderstanding or intention and no one was aware of this fact. It was up to me to bring this to the fore of everyone's attention in this way, when the time was right.

The job was reasonably well paying, and the company I worked for provided care on a private basis. This intimate hands-on work was invaluable, although a totally different set of skills were required. I was responsible for the most vulnerable of people on an everyday basis.

I used the time wisely whilst with them, and I used to ask them about their childhoods, any effects the Second World War had on them, and whether they were old enough and could remember this time from their childhood memories. They all seemed pleased to be able to have someone genuinely interested in them, so it was a well-suited level of information and well-being exchange.

I gleaned invaluable knowledge as well, furthering the development of my wisdom bank. My abilities allowed me to work well with the more difficult clients. I could look into their pasts to see how they had got to being in the positions they were in. I had a way of not letting their idiosyncrasies get to me, as I could look behind the persona the person presented to the outside world.

I also learned how to talk to people in everyday language, which had escaped me until then. I was also able to get some experience of talking to a group of residents in a women's refuge, as the manager of the company I worked for knew the work that I did and had contacts at the refuge, and she asked me whether I would mind going in and giving a talk to them.

This was invaluable too. It gave me real, hands-on experience with the people that needed me the most in the way of emotional control issues. I went there three times, and the ladies were grateful for my input. I helped each of them find purpose and a way to think forwardly in these sessions.

I had been doing this job for eighteen months when, in 2018, a totally unexpected doorway was opened up for me, pushing my boundaries in a way I would never have imagined.

Things were not going as well as I had hoped in my personal life, and I knew there was something I was not seeing that was escaping me in my conscious understanding of events. I had gone to visit one of my daughters and was explaining that I couldn't see something—that there was something missing. At this point it would be worth adding that my children knew of my path pretty much as soon as I did.

I do not discuss details with them; I am just there for them in any way I can be, with advice if they ask, and with gentle guidance if they do not. I also just listen so they can bounce their troubles and inspirational thoughts off me without judgement. I am Mum to them and Nana to my grandchildren, and their paths have not been easy either.

Anyway, as I said, I couldn't get over this feeling of missing something. Now, one daughter of mine has been to university and has a master's degree, against all odds of adversity to stop her achievements. She said, "Mum, you are forever writing and researching. Why don't you go to university?" As she finished saying these words, all the uncertainty and all the personal horror I was going through collapsed like a house of cards.

The frequency I had been used to tuning into suddenly came back at full volume. I had dearly missed my time away from the universal connection, and it was clearly time to return to the fold. I had always maintained my personal guidance frequency, but the frequency which was slightly to one side of this I didn't access whilst doing the physical work of a carer. If I had used the strength of this connection for everyday use not connected to my higher purpose, this would have interfered in an adverse way for me. It would have appeared as an overinflated ego and would not have helped me one bit; it would just have drained my energy.

Anyway, back to the point of the story regarding this suggestion of university. I had always had a mixed reaction about university. It certainly had never been my bag! I had left school at fifteen with no qualifications, and exams scared the pants off me. But what I *had* learnt about was instinct and intuition. I didn't think I stood a chance of being accepted at the age of sixty-four years old, but I did agree to find out.

I made one phone call to a university in the area closest to me. On that call, I briefly explained my experience in life with helping people, and the types of situations I had helped with. I kept the call reasonably brief and spoke with passion. I was told to expect a more in-depth interview over the phone, but that didn't happen. Within four days, I had been accepted for entry.

I gave my notice as a carer and set off on a totally new, unexpected adventure. This sorted out my focus in a way I could never have done, with clarity on my professional life and personal life leading me to one conclusion—that I was to get myself back up to the discipline that I needed for the final run-up to producing this book for you to read.

10

LISA'S STORY

There is one person I have not talked about so far in this book, because she deserves a chapter all of her own, and this is Lisa. Amongst all the women and men that I have met and counselled over the years, she is living proof that this new way of teaching and learning about the true you, works. It isn't just a theory! When I start my rounds of talks, she will be, for some of the time, accompanying me so the audience can ask her questions.

We have discussed this and she thinks it would be amazing for her to answer questions on how she has used the wisdoms she has gleaned from this new, exclusive form of study, where the only person you need to study is yourself.

Her story goes back to late 2002, when a chance meeting with someone led her to come to my house within two days, as she was trying to end her life and no end of counselling sessions was doing anything to assist with the emotional trauma she had gone through in her life. She had two children who were on the verge of being taken into care because of her inability to cope with life. She had been in trouble with the law, was a drug user, and suffered from alcohol abuse. She could not read or write very well.

Her personal story was tragic. She self-harmed from a young age, had no one to talk to, and was encouraged to leave the family home at the age of fourteen by her stepfather. When I read her story to the ladies in a refuge centre for abused women, they had tears rolling down their faces. I must stress this was done at Lisa's request to try to encourage the ladies to listen to what I have to say, because she knows more than anyone that if you stick to the path of wanting to turn your life around, this will happen.

Lisa was twenty-nine when she came to see me. We spent four hours together, and some of that time was spent going out to grab some fish and chips and eating it by the beach. In those four hours, I gave her an alternative point of view of her life. She totally understood that all of her experiences were going to be for her benefit in the future and that the wisdom of all these things would surface. She relocated to get out of the area that was keeping her in a continual cycle of self-sabotage.

It is now eighteen years since we first met, and she passes on her wisdom to those that she feels need a nudge. Like me, she has understood that people will let you carry them if they have an opportunity to lean on you, so she has learnt the signs of when to let go, but she will offer guidelines if asked.

From that point in 2002, at her lowest point, she now has a life worth living. She realized that she could change the story of how society looked upon her.

She done a basic course on mathematics and English. She was accepted to do voluntary work in a youth club, as her expertise of understanding teenagers was a natural instinct within her, with her having been a teenager herself. This work she did for quite a while, and it eventually paid off when she applied for a job in a school for troubled teenagers as a teaching assistant, which she still holds.

She understood patience and tolerance but knew the moral code that we abide by. This allowed her to know when to chastise the teenagers so that their souls could hear. We are friends now, and she asks for advice only if she feels she hasn't got the right answer to a problem, because she can *feel* it isn't right; she knows there is a better understanding which she can't see at the moment.

She totally understands universal law, but she does not always know how to apply it for the best interests of all concerned. This is a continual learning curve, even for me. New situations evolve, and so do the answers, in this ever-changing world that we live in at the moment. The important thing is to always be mindful that there might be a more harmonious way to deal with things if an answer doesn't continue to sit right with you.

Lisa now has her own home on a mortgage, whereas at one time she was living in temporary accommodation. She has her own car, whereas she couldn't even drive when she met me. She has a steady job, and she has found true love by applying the rules on behaviour from her own self-worth level, which have become a way of life for her now.

She applies the same standards within all of her relationships, including that with the man she loves. She will not settle for anything less from him. Lisa will admit freely if she feels responsible for any misunderstandings that have caused friction, and she receives the same level of respect from him. There is total honesty between them, which they have worked hard for, and they have a relationship that many would envy. The wedding is booked, by the way!

She is not afraid to speak her truth to stop someone trying to overpower her. She removes herself from a situation rather than meeting confrontation with like for like. She has such a big heart, and she can now use it to its fullest advantage for loving and giving to those whom she cares about and those who have shown respect to her on a level of trust. She will not allow abuse of any kind to enter her life; she can spot it a mile away.

She used to use her emotion for self-destruction, as she gave her trust to those that didn't deserve it—those that had no moral conscience. She did not know that the pain she was feeling didn't actually belong to her. She was carrying the emotion of everyone in her life because she wasn't taught any worth other than to be there for the use of others' intentions to make themselves more worthy than she was of her trust and affection.

Put another way, she was carrying the pain of *others'* wrongdoing towards *her*, which is what those that are troubled do before they understand universal law. Lisa had unwittingly given them the right to use her will at their bidding to increase their own self-interest at her expense, because she didn't know, like most women, how to understand its methods and terms of use. No one does. Lisa was my first full-on client that kept in touch. I do not know whether the others I have helped along the way have kept the morality of the law intact. If they haven't, they put themselves below the entry level, and they probably will have lost the most precious gift life has to offer. The more you are willing to learn and abide by the rules of morality and honour, the more you will understand and increase your well-being. Once you have reconnected to your soul, it will always take care of your needs.

11

THE FINAL RUNDOWN

I have since understood Lisa's ability to go from strength to strength was my confirmation from the metaphysical world that everything is now in place, and it is the advocacy of the fifth dimension that will help to continue my quest to reconnect people with their souls so they can take full advantage of being incarnate. The fact that I went beyond the mission of soul reconnection to find the original reason why it was necessary, has only reinforced my knowledge and given to me the proof that I needed for it to make sense to me. It was a sort of 'closure' of sorts.

I couldn't bring it to you, even though I knew all my research was sound, if it did not *make sense to me*. Finding the link to religion and then being shown where it started to go wrong, was the biggest breakthrough for me to complete the cycle of events. Although I did not doubt its validity, there would have been a weakness present—a point in time when I could have totally misunderstood the bridge between the world of human conduct and behaviour, and the metaphysical world of universal law, and I could have used the wrong 'frequency' to make that bridge strong.

The only way to ensure perfection for *you* to understand it, and me to confirm it, was to ensure that the natural law of *time* was and always will be observed, because *time* is our dearest friend. It can also be our worst enemy if we are pushed into making decisions that we are not ready to make. This is where increasing one's natural awareness as to what is right for you on your instincts and intuition step in. This will happen when you commit to being part of this new understanding—the original guidelines for the human race.

The importance of insisting that these rules be your guide will also give you the confidence to wait until you are ready to make decisions in your own time regarding things that are important to your soul's worth. You will feel uneasy if someone is trying to overpower your will. I have been shown what it looks like when someone is using stories to drag you into his or her world. This happened to me whilst I had a visitor in my home that I had doubts about his authenticity of behaviour and intentions. He was doing his best to get 'inside my head' and encourage me to see only good things about him, and for me to let go of the disrespect that he had shown towards me.

It is best described as black tentacles heading your way. I could not physically move out of the way at this point and he was talking and getting the attention of others in the room but aiming the tentacles at me as I was the one the story was aimed at to get my attention and compassion through *gentle, unseen persuasion*, I pushed them back to him with my mind. I did so not with force, but just gently, to match the speed with which they were being sent out. I did this so as not to cause too much of a change in the metaphysical airspace. I didn't stop until I made sure the tentacles were back with him, and I left the energy there until the subject could be naturally changed because he believed his mission was accomplished.

No law was broken, but this is how we all get used—by giving away our will without realizing it. False methods of trying to access our natural compassionate ways, needs to get you to agree with something that may not in your best interest. For example, the methods used might encourage you to give your money away, but they can also involve getting you to agree with something that makes you feel bad or awkward if you don't agree. Both are forms of manipulation.

Persuasion, manipulation and emotional blackmail can be allowed under the present rule of universal law, as you have agreed to give your will to something without checking out the validity of the total message—the real truth of why it is necessary to give your precious free will, which is yours by right, away. If you recall, this was the original bad call. We agreed to listen to the rules as they had apparently been dictated by God. This I don't doubt as being true, but as I have already stated, when the message was interpreted, there were missing elements in its delivery—assumptions that were wrong. This, in fact, is something that I, too, have tried hard to cover in this book. People's viewpoints differ so much. I have had to trust that my work and my words are to be taken as inspiration *only* in an attempt for you to make sense of unhappiness and know that no one alive today is the real cause. But we cannot continue to live in a community of blame; we need to be sure that the story of us can change. Words are everything that being human is all about, but once they are written, the interpreter becomes the reader as to the intention of the text.

Socrates, the great philosopher, knew this wisdom—that once one has written down one's words, those words can be misinterpreted; the emphasis put on the wrong word at any given time can change the point of the original intention. This is why he would never write anything down. He used only the spoken word. This is one of the most profound stories I have learnt from history books.

Socrates met his death by drinking hemlock, in a forced self-execution by the ruling powers of the day, who did not like the attention he was attracting or the truth he was talking about to those that listened to him. He was trying to open their minds up to truth, just as Jesus did in his way, and just as I am doing in my way. I am using a different method than they did.

In our time of free speech and science, I am calling on our lives as living proof and using our history to back up my story. The science of it is that a new way, the original concept, has not been widely used by us, as no one knows of its existence. It's like a spiritual vaccine has finally been produced to help us rid this world of wrongdoing.

This living proof has been provided by the soul plane, which no one denies exists. As to the best of our knowledge and belief, the soul is everything in pretty much every religion. The *existence* of a soul is not disputed. So the vaccine which has been produced is metaphysical. It is the opening up of the extended, original versions of our souls that is written of within these pages on personal discovery. My words are the clues for you to increase your own connection to your soul.

I am attempting to give you *sound reasoning* to not dismiss this version of effective research, as I have included the little known of element of universal law. The only guidance we have ever been given until now is from religion, and it has not given credence to the existence of universal law in any way as an entity in its own right, even if its purpose is to back God.

If we had been told of this early in our understanding, it would have made more sense and would have ensured that the rules to live by were known and abided by, because one wouldn't want to suffer the repercussions of going against the rules. God, in his own right, is the Father. His role is allowing compassion to be the ruler of the intention of our deeds.

His perception of honour, in its purest sense and understanding, is why he has allowed me to bring this to you now. He *is in your conscience* whether you accept that or not, because that was the deal when the formation, the inception of intelligent human life, was instigated. He believed that we would see the true worth of our individual lives *in time*, and his honour is what holds him in this light.

He won't let you down. It is not in his interest to do so, so he will always be there for you when you can't be. At the point when you believe all is lost, ask for help. The flip side of this, in case you were thinking this was turning into a text of preaching, is that he cannot insist that you will see yourself as part of the "belonging" that is available to you. This is why he has been held prisoner in your mind—because his honour means that he has failed in his commitment to you, and there would be no other way that the human race, as a species, would exist. We would then be game for any strong mind to overpower, and no father would want that for his child. So the ruling element of compassion makes sense on many levels. It is a make-or-break component of our psyches. The bottom line of this is that compassion is the key to all things, for the self and others, and this is the responsibility of God.

But on the other hand, he needs your permission to help you and to be there for you when things are too much to bear or when you cannot go any further with the thought pattern that suggests the only way out is total destruction—either mentally or physically, or both. As this element of compassion has become so sparse in our everyday lives (apart from those that try to use it for financial or personal gain), universal law is stepping up its role so it can be seen in its own right as an element that will bring balance into the emotions for those that choose a new balance with a scientific analysis that can make sense to them.

This needs to happen so you will understand why compassion is so important and so you will allow it back into your daily life. Universal law exists and is present, whether you believe in it or not; it sees everything—every detail, every decision, and why you make your decisions—according to your intention. The only other element you need is determination to succeed in making this your new benchmark; this will allow you to give your will freely to accept its presence of what's happening on the deeper levels of your subconscious.

I will now talk about compassion and why we often overlook its importance. First, to make this perfectly clear one more time, the two factors of God and compassion are the same; they share the same frequency. You don't have to believe in a god; just believe in the ruling emotion of compassion, and your way will be harmonious and will be everything that is desired for you. If God is everything to you, this is the level you need to understand in humility to help him regain his honour so he can be released from the grip of everything else that man holds in this world as important, overriding your own conscious choices before you have had time to consider options that could benefit you better than the ones being thrown in your face.

Compassion is found through *time*, the other element of expression that we rarely afford to anything worth looking at closely. We are always being rushed along, our choices being thrown in our faces for immediate decision-making, usually with a deadline attached so we don't have a chance to bring our instincts into play and think for ourselves.

If we believed in universal law, anyone trying to hoodwink our decisions for self-gain and use our will for his or her best long-term interests would not win for long. Universal law cannot intervene in your decision to give your coveted will away to whomever you choose. But your *choices* might be different if you knew that you would suffer the *consequences* of your choices.

This means that even if you didn't give yourself enough time to think about the long-term benefits *and* the possible fallout of your choices as they grow to a fruition not in your control or not in accordance with your intention, you would still be liable for the *effect* (the result), as your choice was the *cause*. Taking responsibility for your life and the decisions you make is the new way.

The disappointing truth is that it was the *original* guideline for us all to know about. Ask yourself these things: What is your *intention* regarding the decisions that you make? What is the ultimate *purpose* of your actions? Whom have you / do you put your *trust* in? Do you believe that your *will* is freely given at all times? How confident are you that you live your life completely and utterly under the laws of morality and honour and have ultimate respect for your soul's needs and those of others, whether or not you personally know them?

The only guidelines we have had have been given through religion, and it appears to have been a watered-down version. Why this was done? Do we have to assume this was done by default? Or perhaps it was intentional, done with the thinking that man would just do as he was told and that God would pick up the tab for anything that wasn't understood as true under the eyes of universal law.

This in itself is a truth, but it cannot keep happening, as no lessons are being learnt for any true worth. If someone else is always paying the price, why do you need to abide by a moral code? If you knew everything you did was indeed being observed by an independent judiciary system, would you think twice about your conduct towards yourself and others?

My original understanding that God has been captured by man

now makes sense. He has indeed been paying the price for his faith and belief in mankind to do the right thing. His role has always been one of compassion, which has been abused by not being seen in its truth of intention and purpose. It has not been used to help growth through learning for ourselves—the unique quality of compassion.

We have picked out bits that suit our needs to make us feel whole again in order to replace a guilt of some description. The word, the true meaning of compassion, is known by a select few. Many have learnt how to *use* compassion for gaining something that is wanted, using the wrong intention and purpose as the driving force. All that is done in such cases is to treat the *effect* of any pain or suffering, as the *cause* is not something that can be tackled with the knowledge that rules our senses at the moment. God's original version would have never seen women and children abused in such a way, for that would be going against *his* self-worth and purpose of being a father. Man is supposed to emulate his version of being a father, not pick the bits out that suit man so that he has *power over the emotions* of women by manipulation or emotional blackmail.

Love cannot be given by force. It has to be a natural flow, as we all know. But look at the world we live in and how a lot of women are treated from birth just for being born female. In some cultures, marriage is a way for us to be used, and our natural capacity to love is expected to allow us to find a way of accepting this role, while men feel hard done by and may feel the need to take mistresses or second wives.

We are expected to be grateful that we are being provided for, while our emotions are abused and used. The proof is there. God, who is our Father, would never want that for us as his daughters. All the proof you need is there to be seen. God has had faith in man to understand its failings, but man continues to believe the lies of self-supremacy so the worth of his conscience remains intact. Man never faces the responsibility of the misconceptions of the past. He has never needed to.

Occasionally we raise our heads in different ways to fight what we know is wrong from time to time, but all that happens is that man pats us on the head and gives us some form of "equality" that we take as winning. The proof is there all the time if you know where to look for it. It's all just sidesteps to keep us away from an undeniable truth that needs to surface.

But we have never really gone as far as I am going now to lead us all to the front of the pack *equally* with man in such a way that we can ensure harmony. We have the ability to be compassionate and giving as a *natural response*, but it has been *expected* of us until now, and we have complied, not realizing what we have been doing to ourselves, which is a totally different frequency.

This has made us cut off from our natural, flowing energy, and we are going to have to learn how to retrieve it. That's what I have done, so I know it is possible. I was hard, cut off from my natural femininity. I had to survive, as I have explained, as we all do—having to do things we would rather not have to. But the real power of our gender—and I use the word "power" with caution, as it is a word of the mind, is our ability for true compassion that flows from the heart in its true form, and we can regain our natural flow.

One you have understood the freedom of the heart this brings you, you won't want it any other way. We were not given the truth in a way that made sense to us regarding taking responsibility for our actions (including giving away our right of natural protection) because the leaders of our spirituality took control of our worth, believing they were the link between both genders and God.

We are now able to have trust in that decision that is being given to us to change the world in a way in which only we can change it. We have paid the price, and it is now our natural right to be given the same opportunity that was given to man, to see if we can do better. Women have always had a natural link; men had to learn how to achieve it. This has been totally overlooked. Instead it was expected of us, ladies, to take responsibility for man's failure to search for a higher truth. In truth, man didn't see what was wrong with his version, and so it has been for millennia.

The tunnel vision of this thinking is absurd, but look at how long it has been this way whilst we have had no option to believe in this. We gave our *trust* to man that this is how God feels we should be treated—to feel grateful to man for "providing" for us. God has suffered the price of this, and I can now say, based on my own personal experience, that no man who dares to treat me like an object will get away with it.

I have never had to do anything in this way. The men I have been wronged by have always come to a sticky end in a way deemed appropriate for the abuse that has taken place. Such is my own faith in God and the protection of universal law, which run alongside one another to see that justice is always carried out. Feminism, in its form of fighting man on his own terms, is the forerunner of this new teaching involving the fifth dimension and my work within this realm.

We are now picking up the thread that was left here by Jesus and by all other gurus that have known the true way. But the bigger picture of this is that we are fighting our own natural instincts to be honoured for being who we are, respected in our own right, and to prove we are more encompassing in our natural state of femininity. We can't all be full-on warriors for the cause in a physically confrontational way.

This is another understanding for why universal law in its own right needs to step in. Jesus did his bit to make this possible for us to do. His showing that it was known in his time allows us to follow with his work on our own behalf. The frequency that he was tuning in to, I have realized, is the same frequency I tune in to. As he said, "What I have done so can you." So I am following in his footsteps and attempting to explain the science behind the reasoning of my findings in the best way I can, that you may understand the validity of what I say in our time of science and proof being required for everything.

I have instigated this as I have uncovered this truth, so it is now operational and ready to help restore natural law through your intention to learn the rules and abide by them. In other words, take responsibility for your conduct.

To recap (using an alternative viewpoint to explain the same facts), as the female gender, we have an automatic connection with

God. We have been abused regarding our natural instinct to talk to him using our own natural intuition, as it has been accepted that man believes he has the right to overpower our instincts. We have given our will to religion, which was dictated, by the hand of man, to have the power over our own personal connection. By a common understanding, man has believed it is his right, which he needs to use, to keep himself "pure" in intention and deeds. We have consistently paid the price for this throughout history. There is enough proof of this in history books.

So we need to reclaim our connection and ensure that we alter destiny for us and our children by calling upon universal law to step in and help us do this. It is there, ready and waiting for you on the feminine protocol frequency—the bridge to the fifth dimension. Remember: it is still within your spiritual DNA to be able to activate this; it is just re-education that you need, ladies. And this re-education is what I have instigated.

Further proof to give to you on this frequency of connection highlights the way there is an increasing amount of harm and abuse being done to children. This is because raping, taking the power from women (through fear), is not enough any more. The pure connection that we have always had has been "raped" from us spiritually as well as physically, to such an extent that we do not satisfy the needs of men who think like this. We must save our children from this increasing abuse, which is leaving them with a lifetime of altered truth on what life is about.

We can change that now, and that's all that matters. I think I have exhausted every avenue of explanation I can find to hit a nerve—that "tweak" inside of your mind—to allow you that thought, that chance to explore in your own way what I say could be true. It *has to make sense* to you on a level that only you know of, as our experiences of who we have had to become in this world to survive are different for every one of us. But the message is the same for all of us on one level.

That code of morality, good manners, honour, and respect applies to each and every one of us. It can do no harm to bring this into a conscious awareness for all on following a code of conduct. It is how far away are you from that code of conduct that will help you decide how far you have fallen from your true self-worth.

Okay, just one more understanding of the same truth.

Religion affects a lot of people's ways through its teaching; that is where the first rules of morality went wrong. Respect and honour, if kept at their highest levels, would have protected women and children without my work being necessary. Why? Because universal law takes care of its own. It ensures everyone is answerable to his or her own soul, and every soul is answerable to the universal consciousness. There is no escaping that. But we have been kept from knowing the truth of the rules of this universal, all-seeing law, which works through the conscience. There is clearly a way for those that do harm to others on a soul level of getting away with that.

This is further proof that the true rules have been kept and used for personal gain on a lower frequency that we are told is the *only* wavelength available on which our souls may be heard, and on which retribution is available. Those that know this use the innocence of children, as they give their trust to abusers. If for no other reason, this is worthy of the fight within your own code of conduct to change the way it has been for the perverted minds that think they will get away with their behaviour, because there has so far been no way for anyone to bring these depraved minds to justice, and they know that.

It has to be a universal law, because this law sees all, without words that can be craftily used. *This* is the level of communication that I am now able to tune in to, and there will be no stone left unturned to ensure that the safety of all vulnerable souls is paramount. Your support on the soul level is part of this campaign. Believe you have the power to assist in this change, and you will have it.

God, universal law and not forgetting the help of Goddess wisdom, believes in you to be part of this massive shift of awareness we need to ensure all will be brought to justice. You may not get to know what will happen personally, but just know it will happen. Have faith that this will be achieved because you were willing to believe in something using your trust, free will, and the purpose of your intention in your new commitment to succeed in your quest.

Just know that your reward will be in the new life you will enjoy as confidence and soul worth become paramount in your life, and you won't settle for anything less.

I am here to help *anyone* who wants to hear, understand, and abide by the rules of universal law, this law being to have good manners, morals, respect, and honour, and the implementation of those. That is it. How simple could that be—and how hard to achieve, in reality, is it? It would not have taken me twenty-five years to bring it to you if it had been that simple. My experiences have been that everything has been thrown my way to stop me, put me off, and try to convince me that it's me that's got it wrong and that there is nothing wrong with the way things are.

I have been offered good-paying jobs which would have set me financially for life, but it would have been breaking my moral code of having taken an oath to do all I could to bring this knowledge to you, and I could not accept that. Anything that would detract from my cause would have possibly made me lose sight of how important you are to me, on behalf of your own soul. So my life has been a struggle financially, and I have been at points where I have lost everything, but I am rich in a world I really care about—the one that matters and affects our everyday mental health and well-being. That is the world it would be nice for all of you to belong to, and that was my pledge to all women: to know what I now know—or at least know where to find it.

For the sake of your children and those who have yet to live a life on earth, please consider your verdict on whether *you* find it worth responding to this plea from *your* soul, resulting in a pledge from the universe to be there for you, walk with you, and care for your needs alongside your God—as indeed shall I. Hearts and minds, emotion, and logic will then work in unity for the good of all.

Universal law is coming into its own, and the understanding of this is available throughout this book. We have an opportunity to have well-being restored within our world. I am here to make sure everyone has an opportunity to hear of that. My message, my teaching, is here for anyone that wants to listen. I have heard the cry from your soul and have responded. If you hear it too, then that's two of us that are working in your corner for you to succeed in a way that has never been done before.

The future of the children is in your hands now. Don't wait until your dying day, when it will all be too late to change things.

Feel my passion, hear my words, and hear the voices that cannot be heard. I do. For twenty-five years I have been hearing yours. It is time for change. Let it start with you for your family. Write down your wisdoms. Share the moments that would make a difference in your family. Be truthful and honest. Tell them it's my fault if you like! But do something, any small thing, that will make you aware that you now belong to this new movement to save the world form oblivion, quite literally. Spreading the word, talking about this book and my work, would be an amazing start. It doesn't matter how you do so or what people think; just talk about it and the possibility that I might just be right!

I am appealing to that soul sister within you to pull together as has never been asked of you before. I want you to be part of a massive campaign to ensure that all the pain, torment, and frustration of women since intelligent life came into existence on this planet gets put into balance. I stumbled across this information because life just didn't feel right the way it was being dished up from me. I felt a gut reaction to search where I wasn't wanted. But what I found out is for all of us.

It doesn't matter whether you think of this as an opportunity for personal growth, an opportunity to find a peace of mind that you have never found before, or an opportunity to help the children of tomorrow by being there for the women of today.

What you do with that truth is up to you. All I ask of you is that you not disrespect or dishonour the information within these pages. If it does not ring true with you, that's okay. There is always the right time for anyone. But please do not make it harder for those for whom I have worked so hard to provide a truth that works on a troubled mind and that makes sense to them when no other truths have worked. That could be you one day, needing help desperately as your life is turned upside down in a way you could not have foreseen was going to happen, and unable to find a way out of your misery and torment.

So even if you do not agree with the information in this book for some reason, I ask you to please keep an open mind and do not dishonour your soul's worth or the well-being of others that are waiting for my words and have been doing so for a long time.

Sisters don't always agree; they are just there for each other in times of need.

12

COMPASSION AND THE LINK TO SOUL WARRIORS

I have been asked to include some more direction in assisting you in understanding the help you are entitled to have, and how to access it. Read this with your logical, intelligent hat on, and it will guide you to the emotional integrity that will forevermore keep you in control of your emotions without having to cut them off or block them permanently.

Understanding compassion is the key to your answers, your problems, and your troubled mind. Compassion has to be allowed from one soul to another on a non-judgemental basis. This in turn will dissipate fear from the mind that could interfere with your choices.

If you have to make choices that do not include your own well-being, consciously acknowledge that choice out of fear, not your own free will. Ask for inner help with resolving having to make that choice, which you know is against your better interests. This will invoke universal law to get involved. (More depth of understanding on that is provided below.)

I have channelled this directly from the soul plane. For the first time in history, they have matched a call from someone who could see further than what had been instilled into them from the beginning, consciously. Universal law has seen fit for me to cover all aspects of soul abuse and has allowed an army of souls—willing and signed up to help me help you—understand that there is a better way to live.

They will assist you in finding answers to your problems, as they all have collective experience on resolving the disharmony that resides within your senses. There are many famous, well-known people that are helping, including royalty, gurus, and warriors of all descriptions. They all want to see justice regain its rightful place amongst us to be the ruling component of our psyches, where injustice has ruled for far too long because no one knew how to access the realms where the *real* authority on behaviour and conduct dwells.

Now what this means to us (you), in down-to-earth language, is that the army (the spiritual DNA that came to me on the top of Mount Sinai) consists of all the souls I have just mentioned, in a form you would not generally see, but you will *feel* their presence. Ask a question inwardly, and usually within three days you will have your answer. Keep your mind open to the feminine protocol frequency, and this will happen.

Let me explain the balance of help that is happening here. All those souls that were never heard in their own right whilst incarnate (living a life on earth) will have an opportunity to speak through you, alleviating their pain and, to a degree, torment of not having been able to live the lives they believed they would live, because they were controlled by society and its blind eye that has been used to the plight of women.

Obviously there are men as well who have died having not been heard, and they are also present in this spiritual army to help men acknowledge your new personality and to help with the changes that need to happen. This army does not take prisoners, but it will assist all that search for wisdom through patience, tolerance, and the will to succeed in finding compassion for the self and others as the ultimate purpose.

"Compassion" is just a word. When you realize that it means treating others with the same tolerance and patience that you would like to be shown to you, it makes more sense. Taking responsibility for your responses and honouring your decisions and the decisions of others will keep the balance. If you know a particular decision is not wise, and you inform another person (whomever it may be) that if this were you, you would not do that, yet the person still insists on the decision, say no more and let go of the *responsibility* of the outcome.

As soon as you let go of the responsibility of the outcome, you are breaking away from the other person's will overpowering yours. You have internally disconnected from being involved on a *spiritual* level with any involvement of outcome. It is this separation of the spiritual level that will stop you from getting emotionally dragged into another's decisions if things go wrong as you foresaw they could.

Do not speak of the subject, and do not get involved with any conversations regarding it, but do not be rude or abusive in any way, as that will disconnect your energy stream from the purity of the soul army, and they then will not be able to interfere with the outcome. This takes time to adjust; just ask for help in understanding and in discovering how to be this new person that you are committed and determined to be, leaving you in control of your emotional force.

Your free will becomes yours to use in your senses for your own good and the good of those you love, which includes the well-being of all women, as we are all sisters in this. This has to be the main priority, as we are responsible for the well-being of the children. At the end of that, if men are treating you with the honour and respect you believe you *deserve* because of your new-found self-worth and confidence, they, too, will be given it in return by you from the level of trust from one *soul* to another.

Notice I italicized "soul" there. I am not referring to giving men the right to speak to you with their *minds* and expect you to let life carry on as normal. Be truthful. Tell them that you understand a lot of things now and that your behaviour towards them might change, but it will lead to better times for all involved (or something like that; I am only giving you a guide). That might lead to a conversation that will allow truth to enter your relationship, whereas taboo subjects were previously left unspoken. Give them the same opportunity that you would want if you were them. At all times, in the truth of the highest understanding of justice through unseen truths, we must keep in mind the sacrifices that have been made by so many. We are doing this for them as well as us.

This releases them from their own torment on earth, during which they were powerless to do anything about the injustices that were being carried out towards them whilst they were here. They will know the ultimate prize is theirs—that they didn't die for nothing, and that their lives have counted and are part of this movement, this campaign to return our well-being to be the universal purpose of humanity. I cannot stress this enough. This whole book is an attempt to awaken your senses in order to get you to realize that this not only about you; it is about all women, all children, and all men that have died needlessly because man generally has not allowed wisdom to be the guiding emotion, as wisdom takes *time*, and this is not a virtue men have as second nature.

13

FURTHER UNDERSTANDINGS

To give you the ultimate proof of our capabilities, let me enlighten those that didn't know this. Right from the *conception*, the *inception* of life, did you know that the "male" sperm rushes on ahead to find the egg to be fertilized within the womb and lives only for around twenty-four hours? The "female" sperm takes its time. It can live for three days to give *time* for the egg to reach its correct place and be ready for fertilization, allowing it to outlast the "male" sperm. (This is obviously a very basic explanation of how it all happens.)

So as you see, even nature, from the very beginning, gives us the capability to act with wisdom without words beyond man's capabilities. We don't have to *fight with man*. We can just wait for him to fail through lack of foresight or opportunity. That's the way it is and has always been. Man is responsible for the fertilization procedure, and his sperm dictates the sex of the child, according to the cycle of the ovum.

This is, in a nutshell, the most fundamental argument that is undisputable. It is a fact of life and should be the way we look at ourselves. We have the capability to be wise and have foresight (intuition and instinct), which we all use on a *subconscious* level. What I am here to do is awaken that link between the subconscious and *conscious* levels in you so you are able to understand the *responsibility* of the decisions that you make which shape your destiny.

It is a question of priority, and you have to make your feminine stance, your birthright of being respected and honoured for this, your main concern. That starts with you towards yourself. No longer the victim in all of this, retake your position in your own world with the correct method. Have compassion for *yourself* for what you have allowed to happen to you, because you didn't know any better; and have compassion for *man*, because he didn't know any better either.

But you do know now. It is within the capability of us now to turn our positions in life to positions of strength and honour, because the soul plane, which has always been there, has joined us consciously, as I have explained. Never before has this been possible in this conscious way; it is possible now only through the frequency on which I have forged a road for you to succeed. Any other frequency will not tune in to the *purity* of the soul plane, and universal law's own rules of agreed assistance will not be met. Remember: I have gone on ahead of you by twenty-five years in conscious awareness of my task.

My commitment is to free your will from the denial of its purity of connection that we feel but have never been able to identify. We feel it as unworthiness, lack of confidence, and self-loathing, and we try to deny it further by forming habits that allow us to feel happy for a short time about that denial. That is why compassion and looking for the understanding in your own and others' behaviours are the keys to success, because nobody is truly happy when he or she is not *fully* connected to his or her own soul, which is connected to the soul plane.

The soul plane, in turn, is where the *true expression* of God (not man's version) resides, as I have explained. So following the simple guidelines that I have expressed is the *foundation* of the new you. You also have the army of souls that are there for you and are well versed in any problem you may think is insurmountable. They have been there and done that. They look for honour in having assisted you to carry on with your life, where they could not be heard. Make all human life count, both those still living on earth and those that have gone on ahead to be there for you now.

No one is beyond the vision of universal law. No one can escape its ruling. Remember this, too, the next time a bully approaches you: if you truly commit to this new understanding, everything will be seen in your life; everything will work for you, with you, to help you to grow in awareness of your own connection and strength of character. You will get to see how what you have gone through is a foundation of your life's purpose that was just the training ground to help yourself. This will also allow you to help others in camaraderie as we grow in numbers. The soul plane has arrived on earth and is activated by your calling in times of need. It all makes sense. Everything that I have worked for, and been committed to is finally ready to offer you the opportunity to see the real you—not the you that has been living under the dark cloud of other people's emotions that you have made your own for all of these years.

I can help you with breaking free of the emotional collar that you may feel is around your neck. My email address is at the end of this book. Email me in the first instance for a one-to-one consultation if you truly want to change but lack control over your will at the moment. I also have mediums and clairvoyants on board that have taken the commitment and oath of the feminine protocol and are ready to hear your troubles if you want to share them and get instant guidance.

I have tried to explain that "compassion", as a word, fits the bill of what is necessary to succeed in bringing the senses into harmony. The key to compassion is to *slow down* your present response levels, and it gives *time* to look at the whys of behaviour and conduct. As you unravel the time-space between cause and effect in your own life, you will understand more of the actions of others towards you, and the real reasons you react in the ways that you do.

Our actions are always due to emotional entanglements, loyalties, and emotional blackmail for and by whatever means, which then keeps us in a loop of deception. Always follow the whys and you won't go far wrong if you look at the highest answer that is attainable, being one of purity of thought, and not judge another's journey in life as being the real "them". Just know that you are now alive, awake, and ready to take responsibility for your actions in a way that you never realized before as being important. Do not accept anything less from others than what you would give. Most of what I have expressed here in a fuller version is written in the code of conduct and the spiritual law agreement.

14

SUMMING UP

So much has been covered in this book. I thought it might help if I were to list some of the key elements to remember and add conclusions where it seems fitting to do so to assist in your transition.

1. Moses instigated the rules that he believed God wanted him to write, in the way he wrote them. In his timeline, this was probably what was needed from his point of view, as he had the power of connection to God and wanted his people to feel the same way as he did about the Almighty. He believed they needed rules that were clear and concise, but he omitted to say the responsibility of the outcome would fall on their heads. He makes no mention of cost to the individual if the rules are not obeyed. He also included women in this approach, which God has never mentioned as being part of the rules. It would appear these rules were made in haste, as the emotional well-being of Moses was not good at the time of their writing, having been betrayed in his loyalty to the people, by the people. He did what he believed was right.

2. Jesus tried to put this thinking back into a harmonious way of thinking with a softer, more humane approach—especially towards women. He said nothing bad about women, and again the teachings were directed at men's actions towards

each other and towards the women. He tried to teach women not to be so harsh on each other.

3. Christianity, which was written by man in the aftermath of Jesus, tweaked the words so as to still be able to use our good nature for man's benefit. Our connection to God was always paramount in his mind, so he needed to keep it under control so we did not use the connection for ourselves, as this would have rendered man as below woman, in man's perception. So we are continually ruled by the church (for those that believe in man's approach) under the "guidance' of God, and we are taught to rely on the church for the connection, when in fact it is only the strength of the feminine will that keeps the church going. When you go into a church or holy place, tune in to your own feminine energy of loving and giving, and observe how you feel. All you will feel is feminine energy; this is all the women that go into church and give their will freely in hope of betterment.

4. All other faiths and religions that include God, or the Almighty Father, are based on the original thinking of Abraham and Moses, but it does go deeper than this (see the reminder on this in item 11). It wasn't their fault, but both were biased towards having men possess free will at the expense of women, who just obey what is being told to them as the truth of their lives. Naivety is the cause of all misdeeds, on most levels of communication. There is no judgement; there is just a need of acknowledgement that it is time for change; otherwise I would not have had to spend so long researching all of this from the soul level of communication, which we all talk about but have thus far been unable to understand as to what is wrong and why we are like this. We all know that deep down, we are falling short of our own expectations of ourselves, but we don't know the reason why.

5. The feminine protocol is the modern-day take on religion, and it is also harmonious with the goddesses that have helped to keep women in touch with some of the sacrifices they make

on a daily basis out of loyalty to their husbands or partners, or even society. Chastising as the first rule is no longer the way for keeping your soul with you. Taking responsibility for our actions and reactions needs to become the first priority for us to reverse the culture of blame that runs rife amongst us. Teaching through understanding the whys and why nots has to become the new way, and it will be displayed with a confidence that time will teach. We have not been used to taking time with our own teaching—or learning—in a kind, caring way.

6. Learning with time given for mistakes over misunderstandings is the new way for our emotions to grow and thrive. A new sense of well-being will be discovered by those that take their lives seriously and want to change the story of them. Giving time to yourself has to be the first priority. The logic here is that if you do not think of yourself as worthy of time, others won't either.

7. Do not get bullied into agreements or decisions that you are being rushed into. Slowing down time starts with you. It requires using *your* energy, your will, for you, the children, and the sisterhood so we can all rise and turn this world around through *choice*, not by being told whom and what to believe in, which has been the way for us for millennia as we have been drawn in with emotional blackmail or manipulation.

8. If you do have to do something you would rather not do, know you are doing it not out of choosing; consciously acknowledge that from within, and ask for help in finding a way for this to change into a positive outcome for you. Then let go of the request, knowing you have been heard, and have set the wheels in motion for this.

9. It has been accepted in metaphysical terms that change is needed, and all souls are joining us in a joint effort to give humanity a chance of seeing through this debacle of human consciousness that we call normal. We acknowledge the mistakes of the past, including our naivety in allowing man

to control, although we had no choice in this decision. The foregone conclusion that man's rules were meant for man's conduct were assumed to be known by him.

10. This was also the basic rule of all religion, as God had intended. The fact that man has not consciously recognized our worth is not man's fault; he did not realize what he was doing wrong, even when he was given the option to understand by the guidance of Jesus. Man has been given an opportunity to acknowledge this and has made an attempt, but he still holds the reigns on woman's progress; he does not appear to have it in him to let go fully.

11. We need to lead without doubt from the front, as we have had to follow man's lead from the inception of religion. The story of Adam and Eve, when really looked into with fresh eyes, shows all the markings of why God let man decide his own fate. Adam did not like God's first offering of a mate, who had equality in her own right. Adam wanted a subservient female, so God's choice was changed, as the free will man was promised had to be complied with out of honour. Everything stems back to this first decision made by man, during which religion did not exist; there were then only rules made by man, who needed a platform of conformity. Although this was not seen as such then, this was the precursor of religion, still with the original guidelines of Adam's choices.

12. We are now the story of how things will be for the future, as God's choice is finally being made for the good of all. I needed to reach that part of his honour with which he agreed with Adam to stand by his word. I have taken our case to the highest court of moral obligation and the right to be heard. Man has had his chance to prove his way works—and it doesn't. The flaws, the proof, are all there for anyone to see. All that I have done and suffered over the last twenty-five years was for my appeal that the court of the highest authority listen to our case of moral obligation and serve justice. This book is the proof of the decision made. There is no going back

now for man, as time has run out for him. If you stick by the guidelines and rules given earlier in this book, you will see a difference in your life taking place.

13. As a reminder, the way of the feminine protocol will not interfere with any religion today if that religion consciously acknowledges your worth, but do be aware of your worth. Do not give your freedom of choice away without being prepared to take responsibility for the consequences. You have grown up, and you are learning the real meaning of being born a female in this lifetime, where instinct and intuition are applied from the heart connection to your soul with a new level of insight. This will replace intuition from the mind, which we have been taught to do by man, as that is the way of man. To explain again further, the mind deals with thoughts as its controlling power, not the heart, so it often has tunnel vision for prosperity and will not see where it is leading you to in outcome, which may not be advantageous for you in the long term. The heart (feelings) sees so much more, and wisdom from your soul connection is included for decision-making. This new slowing down of responses and decision-making will make way for soul prosperity that will not fail you, as God and universal law are now included through your acceptance of their authority. As their worth is connected to your worth, this new system of learning through everyday life cannot fail you as you get more adept at knowing that there are no such things as mistakes but only opportunities to learn about things you otherwise wouldn't have to ensure yourself are worthy of your choice. This new-found confidence to take *yourself* seriously will then radiate from you. This is the turning of knowledge into wisdom, which you will learn to look for as well, as it will naturally come to you as you evolve. You can now see everything with a new perspective and attitude.

14. This is the feminine protocol in action. This is for you.

15

CREATING A NEW YOU

I have put together some suggestions that I hope will help you to change your daily routine from possible apathy to looking at yourself with inspiration—a new way for you if you have really hit rock bottom.

For those that have read this book with interest but have never really felt the need for great change, please humour my intention to jump-start those who are more vulnerable to society than you are.

So here we go, with some basic, down-to-earth guidance to point you in the right direction, which I hope will help you in your transformation. This is my final gift of wisdom to you. As women, our femininity is in our appearances as well as our personas. This guidance is inclusive of every woman that wants to change her outlook but does not know where to start.

In my experience, if you look different when you look in the mirror, it can help you to succeed in *being* different. It is all about getting your natural senses back so your intuition and instincts will be connected to your heart in a positive way, not used for blocking your emotion anymore. This is only the beginning. I hope it helps. These suggestions are not for everyone, but they are some things I did; and others collectively assisted, which helped.

Forming your own bridge from where you are to where you want to be might feel daunting. Where *do* you start? These are my suggestions, having gone through this transformation myself. I have listed the best ideas.

The first thing you must have is a commitment to succeed. Have this and you cannot fail.

I have spoken exhaustively about *compassion* throughout this book, but maybe it might help to identify with the word "persecution". Take a minute to think about this word. Maybe look it up in the dictionary to give you further clues. If any of the emotions that are associated with this word make sense to you regarding your feelings, then that will give you the beginning of the understanding of needing compassion for yourself.

It is the first step of enlightenment, but how do you achieve that? "Enlightenment" is the most used word in well-being and spirituality, and I am going to give you some pointers that will definitely help you on your journey. Take your time in understanding the reason you feel the way you do. Look for the pointers that work for you in identifying where change needs to happen to get you to a place of wisdom through this medium.

To implement compassion into your life, start with *you*. Compassion for yourself has to come first, after the journey you have had so far. In the following advice and suggestions, I am responding to the call of those that have no self-worth or wouldn't have a clue on how to find it. There is no disrespect intended in any of this—or, indeed, in any of my words in this book. So, that said and made clear, here are some suggestions.

How about getting some new outfits? Choose a new look for a new you. Go to shops and ask the assistants for help in what they think would suit you. They don't know who you are; they will see you as a woman and will probably love to help out, giving you their advice. Obviously, if you can afford a fashion guru, then go for it! And maybe go into a shop to get advice and then head for charity shops if you can't afford the brand-new clothes.

There are many reasonable brands now. Try some clothes on and get opinions from other shoppers or assistants. I have done this personally many times. People will be honest with you. I have also been asked what I think of something on other shoppers. Don't be afraid of looking for the camaraderie, the sisterhood, in any woman. Get a new coat or jacket—something that is different or makes you feel different. Try to get out of the habit of wearing trousers and trainers all the time. A skirt and shoes are much more feminine.

Have your nails done if you can afford it, or do them yourself, maybe in a colour that is a bit bolder—or, on the reverse of that, one that is subtler than what you normally wear.

Buy a new shade of lipstick. Never the leave the house without applying lipstick! It lifts the face and the appearance of the eyes too!

Changing your hairstyle also has a big effect. Ask a hairdresser to give you advice on what would suit you if you fancy a change. Change the colour, style, or length. Go from straight to curls, or from curls to straight. If you haven't got the finances to do this, how about getting the colour and doing it yourself, with the aid of a friend? Or offer an exchange of natural gifts. Maybe you are good at cooking, making cakes, needlework—something that you could do in exchange for your immediate hairdo!

If you can afford it, treat yourself to a spa day, or at least a facial and body massage.

Learn how to do head massage. Courses are not all that expensive. I teach one myself, using my unique blend of all the techniques I have learned over the years. I have now settled on a de-stressing head massage which really works. Offer to do head massages for friends and your partner. This is also a great way to increase the sensory element of touch.

Invest in some oils and learn about their properties. Lavender is always a good one to accompany a head massage. Also think about doing a foot rub on your partner. Lavender cream or oil is an amazing additive to use. Peppermint oil or cream for the feet will also be a welcome treat. Check that no allergies against using any of these products are present.

Although this is about starting with you, the returned gratitude will feed your soul with nurturing.

Have baths with candles around (always using safety precautions, of course). Battery-operated candles are available and are inexpensive.

Invest in an oil burner or diffuser and try out some various oils that will lighten the air with fragrance. This will be a mood changer too. Research which ones sound good for you based on the affects you would like to see on your mood.

This will increase the sensory element of smell as you find the harmony of what blends well with you.

Before you leave the house, always ensure you are well groomed and you are happy with your appearance. Be determined to keep that smile on your face by smiling within! Sport a hat if you want to feel really feminine! The good news is that you can always find a good hat in charity shops!

Make an effort to get a babysitter and go out with your partner to embrace the new, confident you! Take control of where you go and plan the evening. Know what it is you want to achieve and invoke the best atmosphere to making it happen. Keeping in mind the current covid-19 safety restrictions, you might just have to make this a discussion of what you believe would be an amazing night out,(or a weekend away) and put energy into it ready for when you can make it a reality.

Learn all you can about crystals, essential oils, and try out some spiritual music stations for a change in music that has been produced to uplift your mood. There is so much information on websites now, and books on crystals especially, are always good to have around for reference of individual qualities and use.

On a different note, as we are have been talking about relationships, many have a problem finding the right words to say to a boyfriend or girlfriend when it is time to move on, and they feel such emotional turmoil on how to broach the subject. So I thought I would give you this nugget of relationship wisdom. What I have suggested to those approaching this difficult (and common) subject is this, and it has worked for them. I hope it helps you too with your decision-making.

Say to the other person in a calm manner that your characters unfortunately don't get on in levels that are important to you. Tell the person it is not his or her fault any more than it is yours, but it is something that you have become aware of, so it feels the right time to call it a day, as the gap will only increase and lead to unhappiness for both of you, and neither of you deserves that.

If, however, you are looking for ways to deal with a behaviour of the other person which is proving difficult to deal with (whatever it is that bothers you) but you are not ready for the relationship to end, you could ask if the person could suggest ways that this could be approached, with a view of finding common ground to look at it and deal with it from another prospective. Also ask whether there are any ways of yours that you are unaware that could be difficult to manage. These are just suggestions, but they are made with truth and honesty, with harmonious intent as the outcome.

Back to general advice now!

When you go out shopping, hold the door open for another to walk through; the gratitude lifts the spirit. Also, showing good manners at every opportunity strengthens the will that you choose to be like this—to help others out of free will. Make a point of saying "please" and "thank you" at every opportunity. This also might sound trivial, but it helps you to reconnect with your sense of self-worth and the element of self-satisfaction of soul connectivity with strangers in a wholesome way.

You might want to change to a more wholesome diet, letting your body know it is worth making the change. Increasing your fitness level might also be something that you have wanted to do but could not find the incentive to carry out. You might want to go swimming or join a join a gym if you can.(post covid-19) You will meet new people on equal footing in your own right, increasing your self-awareness for just being you. The people you meet will probably enjoy the opportunity to talk. This will widen your ability to help with confidence, as it a matter of choice rather than something you are being forced to do.

Buy flowers for yourself or go to the woods and find sticks or the odd log that might be lying around and make a home decoration to be proud of. Flower arranging classes are amazing; they don't cost the earth and will show you some great ways to use inexpensive natural items to have in your home. This will increase your senses to enjoying nature.

Also go for walks, watch the changing seasons make a difference to the leaves on the trees, and watching the birds in your garden. Take note when the moon is full, and watch each night as it gets closer to its fullness. Standing outside in its light, talk to it. Ask it to help you and talk with gratitude in helping you in ways you do not yet understand. We are connected to the moon by our femininity. Enjoy this state of natural communication and connection.

Start to look for the signs that make you smile inside—those things that give you a natural gratitude for life, the experience of being you, and what you have to offer this world in your wisdom of life.

Keep your own journal, writing things down when you can to express your emotion. Whether good or bad, say how you feel. You can then pass this journal down to your children, or a loved one, to show what was going on in your life in the past. Make sure you enter the date with every entry. This is a handed-down legacy from you to the generations to come.

These are all things that I have done, and some things are more profound than others in the way they can help you. Do what *you* think is right regarding any one of them. But be prepared for change to happen in a nice way.

If you do need personal help with a problem and are stuck on finding an answer that works for you, I can do one-to-one chat in person. I can also attend a group meeting to discuss methods to overcome issues that you are having trouble with dealing with. Your life will make sense to you; it's just that you have never thought about it like this in the new way of alternative thinking that allows your soul to become involved with your heart and mind. Anything is possible, and it has been so difficult to write everything down here in the written word.

I have given you these pointers to help you start reconnecting with *you*, your soul, in as many ways as possible to empower you with the ability to see life differently. Will this solve your issues straight away? Probably not—at least not immediately. But it will provide you with the *foundation stone* of exploring new possibilities, which you have never given a thought to, regarding finding the real you and what you are truly capable of, loving yourself, knowing why you are worthy of being loved in your own right of being a woman, and feeling the true connection of your God, the universe, and the wonders of natural communication that you are capable of.

I also have available some more in-depth notes to provide you with down-to-earth advice, including tips on how to approach disease and illness, how to stay on top of any fears that are running riot in your mind, and how to increase your awareness of what this frequency of teaching can provide. They go much deeper into the way our minds work, and they provide more answers in a very real way. I have done all I can do in this publication to give you the science, on a global scale, relating to the reason our need to revise our thinking on who we are told we are within our place in society needs to change.

Please email me at thefeminineprotocol@gmail.com with the heading "notes request". They really are a companion and a guide that explains in more detail the complexities of the mind and emotions that are not immediately obvious. These notes will help you to get a real grip on yourself as they challenge your mind further and break through long-held beliefs by educating your thought processes. The cost of these invaluable notes is £10, and they are available as a pdf file. If a hard copy is required, the cost is £20 plus postage and packing.

16

SPREADING THE WORD

To broaden the call for uplifting the spirit of sisterhood, I have a message for business owners, or prospective business owners, who have a particular flair that could help. This could be a light bulb moment for you!

If you want a poster to put in your window, or to show support for the feminine protocol, email me and I can arrange for this. You might want to offer a discount for your products for women. You might want to start a service whereby you can you use your natural talents to help women in the ways I have written about, for a reasonable fee. Come on, ladies! I am sure there are many ways we can re-instigate our natural gifts to help each other in many ways. Get your thinking caps on!

Also, if you are part of an organization that deals with the well-being of your clients and you would like to be committed to the cause of returning a moral code to society and are prepared to take the pledge and oath that we have all taken, let me hear from you!

We are ready to acknowledge your services or products, no matter what business you are in. If you are willing to support and be part of our aim, we will support yours. Posters will be provided to show you can be a trusted business, alongside a certificate to confirm your pledge. More information regarding this can be found in the first instance by emailing thefeminineprotocol@gmail.com with the heading "business support".

I am at the inception of implementing this into society as a whole, as we all are in this conscious way. I am willing to give equal recognition to any person or organization that wants to help raise awareness of the feminine protocol and its aims of re-education of the senses. All you need to do is be responsible for your actions, and this is covered by our pledge of integrity and the universal law statement which you need to agree to. The responsibility is yours to abide by this new code of conscious behaviour and to treat your customers according to the same moral code. This applies to stores (e.g., restaurants, cafes, hair salons, spas) and workers (e.g., car suppliers, plumbers, electricians, builders) of any description; the list is as endless as the opportunities are.

Anyone, in fact, male or female, that wants to join us in our aim of awareness of raising the soul's worth and giving it a say in all we do by our conduct and behaviour towards ourselves and others is welcome. I can also arrange for talks to be given on the understanding of how to implement the feminine protocol to any organization that would like this service.

Let me know if there is something you would like to discuss with me that could help our cause of sharing your talents, or if you are in a job in which you could help the me spread the word by arranging a venue for me to speak at. You could utilize the event to introduce your own products to aid the recovery of the soul connection for all women. What comes to mind for me is oils, crystals, candles, readings, fundraising events, clothing suppliers—gosh, the list is endless now that I come to think of it!

I am happy to hear from anyone, especially if that person is looking for a way to establish a business in the world of helping women with regard to a new look, fashion, accessories, or options related to changing the physical look to promote a change in internal and emotional outlook, which could improve the chances of success for our ladies.

I am sure we can all find a way of encouraging growth through the feminine protocol with inspiration somewhere between us. I will also attend rallies where it is advantageous for the feminine protocol to have a presence. Please email me at thefeminineprotocol@gmail.com with the heading "inspirational talk request" if the cause you are supporting would benefit from some inspirational words of strength and camaraderie. Please note that there is a fee attached to this for expenses.

For those that request it, I am in the process of making available badges, scarves, and wristbands that will show dedication and support for our movement. (Some call it a campaign.) I refer to any descriptions that fit in with inspiration to change. But it is more than that. It is an educational course for the senses first and foremost, with your life as the module to explore. Please contact thefeminineprotocol@gmail.com with the heading "promotional material request".

Also available is a certificate with your name on it to prove your commitment to the feminine protocol and its aims, and as proof that you have been initiated into this fifth-dimensional level of thinking.

Please email in the first instance thefeminineprotocol@gmail.com, with the heading of "certificate request", which confirms your belonging, initiation, and commitment. (Details are given earlier in this book regarding options and cost.)

You are no longer alone. Strength is found in numbers in the most diverse of places. We are all friends in deeds, sisters in our souls. Spread the word in any way you feel comfortable. Let's change the future together, in harmony, through this new education of the senses. It is the ultimate guidance in emotional intellect—the science of intelligent thinking.

Make your own group chats with women that want to hear about my work and the new wisdoms that are being made available through the sisterhood of the feminine protocol. Coffee mornings with a real purpose are an amazing way to increase wisdom and thrash out belief systems amongst you. This is really using your intelligence in the way it should always have been used. The aborigines call this "women's business".

Talk together to increase your wisdom, and if there are enough of you, call me to give an inspirational talk if that feels right. I can also offer ideas on how to start your conversations if you feel inspired to do this but don't know where to start, with guidance notes on how to approach this. Do whatever it takes to support others that have taken the pledge of emotional integrity through the feminine protocol, and they will support you in return.

Take the step into a freedom that allows you to thank your experiences for the opportunity they have provided. Then look for a way to allow them to work for you in proving to you that the feminine protocol's attitude is right as you disentangle your emotions from others. Then decide on the right way to proceed so that harmony of the senses becomes the guiding factor.

All that is needed for you to move into your new-found freedom is for you and your conscience to invoke the connection to your soul through the link that the feminine protocol has provided. It's now your time to take control of the emotions that have held you prisoner for as long as you can remember. Now you have the opportunity to disentangle that hold and choose with new insight on what you hold dear.

You can find a way to make anything work for you; just keep the rules in mind. This is an opportunity of a lifetime that many have had cut short for themselves in an attempt for you to succeed now, with their metaphysical help. All worlds have come together to ensure we don't fail. The choice is yours, as it always has been; you just didn't know who was pulling the strings on your decisions. You do know now.

Make your choice count.

I hope I have helped rattle your brain and caused you to think a bit more on life and how beautiful it could be. I have paved a way for you to get to know yourself in ways you have only doubted until now.

Understand all there is to know about the feminine protocol and you will not be disappointed.

It has been an honour to have had your attention whilst you read my book. I thank you for giving me the opportunity to be part of your life for this moment in time.

I will be your sister, friend, companion, and guide always through the words that you felt were the most meaningful to you.

I did this for *you* because you are worth it. Find your own way to making my words right and you will see the version of you that I see—that your soul sees. Good luck with your own assignment of fulfilling your potential as a woman in her fullest sense!

Your friend and soul sister

Annette x

On the next page is the S.O.U.L Reiki symbol to be used by men during initiation. This symbol represents the 5th dimension, and stands for the *Source Of Universal Love, Law. Logic, Language.* It gets activated during initiation when the guidelines are fully met on the feminine protocol's aims and intentions for the future stability of the human race, the voice of the soul to be heard to instigate a code of behavioural conduct befitting all.

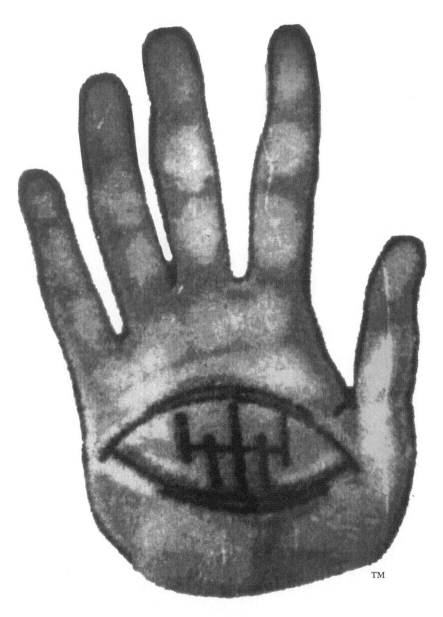

S.O.U.L reiki, turning your why's ....into wisdom'

Printed and bound by CPI Group (UK) Ltd, Croydon, CR0 4YY